STORIES OF THE OCCULT

STORIES OF THE OCCULT

Text by Peter Salmon

An Hachette UK Company
www.hachette.co.uk

Summersdale Publishers Ltd
Part of Octopus Publishing Group Limited
Carmelite House
50 Victoria Embankment
LONDON
EC4Y 0DZ
UK
www.summersdale.com

Printed and bound by CPI Group (UK) Ltd, Croydon, CR0 4YY

ISBN: 978-1-80007-934-2

Substantial discounts on bulk quantities of Summersdale books are available to corporations, professional associations and other organizations. For details contact general enquiries: telephone: +44 (0) 1243 771107 or email: enquiries@summersdale.com.

STORIES OF THE OCCULT

**Supernatural Happenings
and Strange Tales from
Around the World**

JAMIE KING

summersdale

DISCLAIMER

By their very nature, stories of the occult come in all shapes and sizes. The author and the publishers make no claim that any of these stories have any basis in fact. They are merely tales that have enjoyed popularity in the public domain in some form or another. Such stories are reproduced herein for entertainment purposes only and are not intended to be taken literally.

CONTENTS

INTRODUCTION

There are many ways to be a fool, but perhaps the most foolish of these is to believe that the world is as it seems. Across many centuries and across many cultures, people have believed that the physical world we inhabit is only one part of a larger magical realm, in which strange happenings are normal and what we call normal is strange.

From things that go bump in the night, to unexplained disappearances, to apparent feats of magic beyond belief, human history is filled with phenomena that science struggles to explain, but that no rational being can ignore.

So come on a journey into the occult, that mystical place of supernatural phenomena, where twins are reincarnations of their dead sisters, where dolls come to life, where a ghostly wedding feast happens on the anniversary of a bloodcurdling massacre. A place where people mysteriously fall from aeroplanes and aeroplanes fall from the sky, disappear or encounter objects unknown to humans. Where death is always close by and may never be explained. But where death may not be the end, either, if you are lucky – or unlucky – enough to enter another realm.

Where people are cursed by witches, or by destiny, and die in unexplained ways. A place where children turn into ghosts,

ghosts into children and imaginary friends may be one or the other. Behind every doorway is another possible encounter with the weird, the eerie, the terrifying and the occult.

It is a place where a person can be possessed, or a whole family or community, where mass hysteria can rule and devils be found in every pair of eyes.

And that's just the human world. This is also a journey to the limits of all living creatures, and many that are not living. This is the world of cryptozoology, which seeks out all those beasts which science has no name for, beasts that roam not only the Earth but the other worlds that are alleged to exist above, below and in the spaces between. From Gorgons to Grootslangs, deathworms to banshees, you will feel a strange sense of familiarity with these creatures who not only walk the Earth but also walk in dreams. You may have caught them out of the corner of your eye – pray you don't meet them face to face.

The door is open, so come into this world, because this world is your world. You may go about your ordinary business but occasionally stop to wonder why you feel a little strange sometimes, and what that knocking in the walls might be. Take this journey and, whatever you believe now, by the end you may see things a little more clearly...

HAUNTINGS

Hopefully it's just the occasional hand on the back of the neck. Or the vague feeling that you are being watched. A sudden change in the temperature of the room. Or a billowing curtain when the window is shut.

But it seldom is. Usually that's just the first hint that something isn't right. Before you know it, the knocking in the night is getting louder. Things have started to move around the room. You wake up screaming with something on your chest. Blood starts dripping from the walls. And then the room goes black – and the really bad stuff begins.

Ghosts have been with our culture for as long as death has. Be they poltergeists, spectres, ghouls or wraiths, they haunt a space somewhere between this world and the next – and they are seldom happy. Would you be? Unable to find any rest, unable to re-join the humans, they are condemned for eternity to live in the shadow-world. Is it any wonder they are angry?

From haunted houses to haunted castles to ghost ships, a spirit can make its home anywhere, but it is usually tied to the place it died, and it usually died in a horrible way. Those who took its life, or denied it a proper burial, are probably long gone. But you're not. And if revenge must be had, isn't one human soul as good as any other?

CRESCENT HOTEL AND SPA – ARKANSAS

Everyone likes the chance to get away and enjoy a nice holiday, and where better than a hotel and natural spa for the rich and famous? But the luxurious Crescent Hotel in Arkansas is now more famous than anyone who has stayed there. It may well be considered the most haunted hotel in America.

According to legend, while the Crescent Hotel was being built in 1886, an Irish stonemason named Michael fell to his death from what is now Room 218. By all accounts, Michael seems unhappy to be trapped in the very place he met his end. Residents of the room have described doors opening and slamming, the scream of a man falling from the ceiling and, worst of all, hands reaching out of the bathroom mirror towards them.

But Michael is not alone. In the 1930s, the Crescent became a cancer hospital run by the unqualified "Dr" Norman G. Baker. In the hotel's cellar Dr Baker injected his wealthy patients with his "patented cure". The experiments were, unsurprisingly, unsuccessful, with most subjects dying – after which Dr Baker would conduct post mortems. The souls of his poor victims are allegedly still down there, waiting to be healed.

HAUNTINGS

The washers and dryers which now stand where Dr Baker's patients died are suspected to turn off and on by themselves in the middle of the night. A nurse pushing a gurney has been heard at all hours of the day. And more than one hotel guest has reported seeing Dr Baker himself, dressed in a white linen suit, purple shirt and lavender tie. There are no mentions of bloodstains on the suit. He was a very hygienic man, by all accounts.

But the victims of Dr Baker are not the only unquiet spirits at the Crescent. Employees have claimed to have seen Christmas trees moving from one end of the hall to the other, and dining rooms magically set up after being left in a mess, or morphing into a mess after being set up.

One waitress said she saw a Victorian wedding taking place behind her in a mirror, while a cook was sure he spotted a small boy in glasses and old-fashioned clothing skipping around the kitchen. Soon after, he said, pots and pans went flying off the shelves just above Dr Baker's cellar.

Do ghosts attract other ghosts? Or is it a particular location that attracts the dead? Perhaps we could ask those who have stayed in Room 221, where a number of guests have reported being visited by a thin smiling man in Victorian garb, with his head tilted to one side, who disappears as soon as they turn their back. He has even been said to show people to the room, but never stays to receive a tip…

Perhaps he is from one of the couples that are said to dance around the hotel's main salon in the dead of night, forever at a ball they attended when the hotel first opened, forever condemned to dance. Guests have alleged they were startled after accidentally going into this room and seeing the spectres spin round and round. Saddest of all is the tale of a man at a table by the window who says again and again, "I saw the most beautiful woman here last night and I am waiting for her to return." He has been waiting for over a hundred years.

The Crescent Hotel and Spa remains open for business, should you wish to make a reservation. Although the last owner did die in a mysterious car crash shortly after buying it...

THE HMS *EURYDICE*

The naming of ships can be a hazardous thing. Some names which seemed unremarkable at the time have now taken on dreadful significance, like *Titanic*, with its 1,500 victims. Or *Mary Celeste*, found on the high seas completely deserted, its crew mysteriously missing. And there was a terrible irony about the HMS *Arrogant* foundering in 1709, leaving no survivors.

But to name a boat after Eurydice – the mythological Greek woman whose fame rests not only on dying violently but being fated to live forever in the Underworld – seems the height of folly. Perhaps some of the 319 crewmembers who embarked in 1878 from the West Indies towards Portsmouth, England, knew the story of Orpheus and Eurydice before they set off. None could have known that they too would be immortalized in verse – "The Loss of the *Eurydice*" by Gerard Manley Hopkins. Unlike the Greek Eurydice, though, no one could descend to save the crewmembers.

Approaching shore, the *Eurydice* was caught in a heavy snowstorm. As the *Times* reported, "Suddenly a great squall bore down on the bay, blackened with snow and ice circulating at enormous speed. According to eyewitnesses, *Eurydice* continued at full sail with her gun ports open before disappearing in the blizzard. Why she was sailing with open gunports has not been resolved."

Not everyone perished straight away – most of the crew froze to death in the icy waters, or were sucked down by the force of the ship's descent. The captain, Marcus Hare, went down with the ship. He was a devout Christian, and the story goes that he was still praying as he sank below the sea. Why this experienced seaman chose to travel into the storm remains a mystery. Perhaps the Fates drove him on.

Watching from the shore, a three-year-old Winston Churchill would have seen only five of the 319 men picked up, three of them dying before they reached the shore. All other hands sank to the bottom of the sea, where their bones lay with the ship that was their tomb.

If it was the name *Eurydice* that drove it to the Underworld, perhaps the fate of the original heroine, never dead, never saved, also explains why the ship keeps allegedly reappearing. Numerous eyewitnesses have stated they have seen the boat travelling the very waters where it sank. Many a sailor has sighted it at sea, only for it to disappear on approach.

Sailors tell tall stories, of course. But what of Royal Navy Submarine Commander F. Lipscomb, a man of impeccable credentials, who reported that he had to swerve to avoid the ship in the 1930s? The fully rigged ship vanished as suddenly as it had emerged, leaving all on the submarine terrified. Lipscomb was not known as a man given to idle fancy.

In 1997, an even more spectacular manifestation was described by Prince Edward, the Earl of Wessex, who said he saw the boat off the coast of Portsmouth – its three sails still billowing from the storm over a hundred years ago. "I am quite convinced as far as ghosts are concerned. There is something definitely out there, but what it is I don't know," said the prince. Could it be that 314 men still sail the open seas, with Captain Hare at the tiller? Does that mean his prayers worked, or the opposite?

Back in 1878, the *Eurydice* was soon replaced by the HMS *Atalanta*, named for the goddess who protected Jason and the Argonauts as they sought the Golden Fleece. Perhaps names don't matter that much, as two years later it sank, too, taking 311 more lives. Unlike the *Eurydice*, it has never been seen again. So far.

THE UNIONDALE GHOST

It's an empty road, the road that stretches from Willowmore to Uniondale in South Africa. Highway N9 is surrounded by desert and there's not much to see – just the odd guest house, the carcass of an animal or two. Oh, and maybe the ghost of Maria Charlotte Roux.

It was on Good Friday 1968 that 22-year-old Maria and her fiancé Giel, an army corporal, were travelling in a Volkswagen to visit Maria's parents and discussing their wedding plans. She was sleeping in the back when a gust of wind forced their Volkswagen off the road. We don't know if she died instantly, but the passing motorist who found them said she looked angelic and was smiling "like someone who had complete peace with herself".

Giel survived, and a year later married another woman. Is it this that disturbed the peace of Maria Charlotte Roux? That her beau found love with another woman, so soon after her body was buried?

All anyone knows is that eight years later to the day, Good Friday 1976, Anton La Grange was driving his Mercedes on the same stretch of road when he came upon a female hitchhiker with an angelic face. She entered his car and he asked where she was heading. "Porter Street 2, De Lange," the girl replied.

He drove for a while and turned to make sure she was okay. The hitchhiker was gone.

La Grange reported the incident to local police officer, Sergeant Potgieter, then carried on his journey. But then, "Just outside Uniondale, I heard the most chilling sound I've ever heard in my life," he remembered. "To this day I can't tell you if it was a laugh or a scream. It was right in the car, really loud... although I was absolutely alone!"

He went back to the police and they searched the car. No sign. This time Sergeant Potgieter followed. Just outside Uniondale, La Grange said he saw in his rear-view mirror the passenger door open and close. Sergeant Potgieter said he saw it too. "I saw the right rear door slowly open and close," he said, "as if somebody got out."

Potgieter was no stranger to the area, and he suddenly remembered why that stretch of road was burned into his memory. There was that girl, eight years earlier, with the angelic face. Sergeant Potgieter showed La Grange a picture of Maria. She looked uncannily like the girl La Grange had picked up. Where did Maria's parents live? Potgieter checked. Porter Street 2, De Lange.

Four years later, Good Friday 1980, motorcyclist Andre Coetzee was travelling fast on the same section of Highway N9 when he said he felt what seemed like arms slipping around his waist. He looked down and saw a woman's hands holding tight. Horrified, he sped up. He felt three hard whacks on the back of his helmet and the arms disappeared...

Again and again motorists travelling on the N9 have claimed encounters with the otherworldly hitchhiker, always dressed the same and looking to get to Porter Street. She would ride with them for a while across the desert highway, then disappear.

Perhaps Maria Charlotte Roux, wherever she is, is still trying to get home. Perhaps she still wants to discuss those wedding plans.

She was last seen in 1984. Coincidentally, that was the year that her fiancé Giel died – in a separate car accident. Could it be that Maria finally won back her man? Could it be the girl with the angelic face is once again at peace with herself?

CHEAP PROPERTY

No one knows for sure who the first reported ghost in history was. But we do know the Romans described being haunted by them. The great Roman author and statesman Pliny the Younger included a number of ghost stories in his letters. It seems that even then, spectres had taken up the activities they would later become famous for. Pliny describes them moaning a lot and rattling their chains!

In Roman times a house said to be haunted was up for sale, and potential buyers kept being scared away. The great philosopher Athenodorus wanted to buy it, but he was suspicious of the low price. He asked the agent if he could spend a night there and see if there was a problem.

During the night he heard the chains rattling, but instead of running away he went towards where the sound was coming from. There he said he saw an old man with a beard, weighed down by chains, standing next to a pile of bones. Athenodorus understood right away that the bones were the remains of the old bearded man and had him reburied with all the proper ceremonies.

That was the end of the ghost, and Athenodorus got the house dirt cheap!

A SIMPLE CHILDREN'S TOY

"Many moons ago I lived. Again I come. Patience Worth my name. Wait, I would speak with thee. If thou shalt live, then so shall I. I make my bread at thy hearth. Good friends, let us be merrie. The time for work is past. Let the tabby drowse and blink her wisdom to the firelog."

It started as a simple children's toy. In the *Pittsburgh Dispatch* of 1891, the novelty shop Danzigers tempted shoppers with the promise of the Wonderful Talking Board, or Ouija, "without doubt the most interesting, remarkable and mysterious production of the nineteenth century".

If ever a product came to exceed an advertisement's promises – "furnishing never-failing amusement and recreation for all classes" and "forming the link between the known and the unknown" – it is the Ouija board, which some believe has finally allowed the living to talk to the dead.

The new toy was an instant hit, and its popularity was such that some have speculated that the dead had a hand in converting the sceptical to fork out their money. How it worked no one knew. Even the name was mysterious. It was not, apparently, based on combining the French for "yes", "*oui*", and the German "*ja*", but was picked by a ghost when the inventor asked for a suggestion via the board.

Soon thousands of people were sitting around boards, feeling the "planchette" or just a glass slide from letter to letter as their loved ones communicated from the Other Side. Detectives used a Ouija board to ask murder victims who their killer was, while two women murderers in New York claimed the board had chosen their victim. Religious groups expressed outrage at the craze for summoning the lost with these "tools of Satan".

It was on 8 July 1913 that Pearl Curran, a housewife from Illinois, sat reluctantly at a neighbour's Ouija board. A 29-year-old high school dropout, Curran had never written a word outside of the addressing of envelopes for the McKinley Music Company where she had briefly worked. The planchette began to slide around the board as Pearl looked on astonished. "Many moons ago... Patience Worth is my name... Let the tabby drowse and blink her wisdom to the firelog."

Patience Worth explained to Pearl that she came from "across the sea" and had died in 1694. She was a writer from England, a "green rolling country with gentle slopes". She had travelled to America, where she was subsequently killed by Native Americans. She still had many stories to tell.

Over the next 20 years, Pearl claimed that Patience dictated many novels, short stories and poems – 88 of them published in one year. After a time they barely needed the board; like "a child in a magical picture book" Pearl found herself *inside* the stories and simply had to dictate them. "I hear the talk, but over and above is the voice of Patience, either interpreting or giving me the part she wishes to use as story."

Pearl's achievements never led her to financial security. The death of her husband left her with four children to care for. Two subsequent marriages failed. But Patience was with her till the end. Pearl supposedly told her friend, "Patience has just shown me the end of the road and you will have to carry on as best you can." Pearl had not been in ill health, but she developed pneumonia and died soon after.

It seems that the simple children's toy had once again delivered on its advertisers' promise: to answer questions "about the future with marvellous accuracy".

DANCING BEN

In the Old Town of Philadelphia there are a number of historical edifices, such as the Independence Building and the American Philosophical Society Building. In the latter it is said there dwells a ghost who continues to surprise and delight any tourists who are lucky enough to catch a glimpse.

When Benjamin Franklin died in 1790 he had a reputation for sobriety. He was, after all, one of the Founding Fathers, whose Declaration of Independence remains the cornerstone of US law. He was also a writer, scientist, statesman, diplomat, inventor, printer, publisher and philosopher. He still appears on the $100 bill.

So one would expect his ghost to be a sober fellow as well.

Alas not. It is said by a number of witnesses that the ghost of Benjamin Franklin likes to inhabit the statue of him that stands in the American Philosophical Society building.

Others have claimed to have spotted the spectre striding along the street towards Franklin's old house, a walk the great man made many times. Some report him visiting local pubs like the City Tavern along the way, though they remain coy about whether he has a tipple.

Allegedly, one day he knocked a cleaner over in the Society library in his haste to get a book which he obviously needed to check something up in. The cleaner was, it is said, unhurt, although honoured to have "had such a close encounter with" the great man.

But Franklin's ghost's favourite pastime is apparently dancing! Many people have said they have seen him cavort around the rooms, perhaps after getting home from the City Tavern.

What makes all of this even more remarkable is that Dancing Ben does all of this not in the finery in which we are accustomed to seeing him dressed. He does it in the garb of the statue, which, in the manner of statues of that era has him clad in nothing but a toga. So if you happen to be walking in the Old Town of Philadelphia and a portly chap in a toga cavorts past you, or even offers to buy you a drink, don't go phoning the police. Get him to sign a $100 bill!

THE BELL WITCH

At first the family thought it was rats. The sound of gnawing went on all night sometimes, and over time it increased in volume. It was a farmhouse in Tennessee and vermin were not rare, but wherever the family looked for them they found nothing.

In 1817, things had already been getting weird for the Bell family. The father, John Sr., had been in a cornfield when he saw what he thought was a dog, but it had the head of a rabbit. He shot at it, but it escaped. A week later one son had seen a terrifying giant bird of a species no one could identify, which shrieked at him and flew away. Their daughter, Betsy, saw a girl in a green dress swinging from a tree. On approach, she disappeared.

The gnawing sounds started sounding more human. Sheets would jerk seemingly of their own accord from the children's beds and John Sr.'s mouth became paralysed. Then the children began receiving scratches in the night. Betsy was not only scratched but slapped and had pins stuck into her. The Bell Witch was working overtime.

God-fearing people, the Bells asked their neighbours, the Johnsons, to join a prayer session. James Johnson read out loud from the Bible. But when he and his wife went to bed that night at the Bells' farmhouse, their sheets levitated and chairs in the room turned upside down.

As John Sr. grew sicker – his swollen mouth made it impossible for him to eat – the Bell Witch made herself increasingly known. Her name was Kate. When asked what she wanted she replied, "I am a spirit; I was once very happy but have been disturbed." At times she was even polite, especially about Lucy Bell, the mother, who she never terrorized. Kate described her as, "The most perfect woman to walk the earth."

But this did not last long. Soon after, Betsy began courting a local boy. On one occasion, the family watched in horror as Betsy was choked and slapped to the sound of a woman's laughter. The Bells sent Betsy away to stay with friends and the witch followed her – so she came back. Only when she ended the courtship did the attacks stop.

The case became so famous that it is said the president himself, Andrew Jackson, tried to pay a visit, but that his carriage wheels became stuck and he could not arrive. Kate later admitted it was she who had done it.

Finally, John Bell Sr. was found in bed with a vial of poison beside him. Kate informed them she had poisoned him, and he would never rise from the bed again. He didn't, dying a few weeks later.

Finally, in 1821, Kate declared she was leaving but would be back in seven years. In 1828 she did return, but she seemed weakened and only stayed a few weeks, again saying she would be back in seven years. She never returned.

Some say that poltergeists are the result of a girl in puberty causing great hormonal energy – certainly incidents like the Bell Witch seem to cluster around teenage girls. Was Betsy's maturation into womanhood responsible? Was she giving out an energy so strong that she could make objects move and even kill her father? Or is this just blaming women and their sexual energy?

The jury is still out. The Bell family, their friends and neighbours would have no doubt about what happened. Nor, it seems, would the US president.

THE TWO WOMEN OF YOUNG & JACKSONS

Young & Jackson's bar is one of the best-known landmarks in Melbourne, Australia. Opposite the main train station, where travellers to Melbourne have come and gone for hundreds of years, it is perhaps most famous for the iconic painting *Chloé* by the French artist Jules Joseph Lefebvre, which hangs in the main bar.

Chloé is, like most of Lefebvre's paintings, a nude, and its appearance in Melbourne in 1883 so scandalized the good folk of the city that it was removed from the National Gallery and bought by Young & Jackson's. More than one late-night drinker has declared his love for Chloé, and more than one late-night drinker has had his declaration rebuffed. During both world wars soldiers would write home to her, promising they would return to her side. Chloé never responded.

But Chloé is not the only woman to make her presence felt at Young & Jackson's. Those weaving down the stairs of the bar to the street might find themselves quickly sobering up. At first she appears to be a beautiful woman standing against a lamp post, though her nineteenth-century clothing is enough to tingle anyone's spine. Delicate hands show beneath ruffled sleeves. The bottom half of her face is deathly white, but beautiful like a China doll. It is said that one cannot resist approaching her, for her downturned eyes compel even those in a hurry to draw towards her. No one knows her name and some have speculated she is a trick of the light, appearing as she does stood against a lamp post, but there is no doubt that those who have seen the ghost of Young & Jackson's never forget her.

It is only when one gets close that she raises her head in greeting… and then one sees the true horror. Beneath that delicate chin runs an open scar where her throat has been slit from ear to ear. The smile she gives comes not from her mouth, but from this gruesome opening made by violent means. Blood pours down her white blouse in an endless stream. And then she is gone.

Who is she, this mysterious woman? Many claim she is a murdered prostitute, although the fineness of her clothes has made others suggest otherwise. Could she be connected to the nearby Old Melbourne Gaol, where Ned Kelly was hanged and where visitors to the mysterious Cell 17 report being attacked, scratched and bitten by a spirit which remains trapped there? But no women were housed within, despite four being taken there and hanged. Hanging does not open the throat.

Or perhaps, like so many who have died violently, her story will never be known. She is just someone who was chosen to depart this world too soon, and taken too violently to find a place on the other side. Now she stands outside Young & Jackson's waiting for what? For love? For revenge?

No one ever knew Chloé's true identity, either. According to Jules Joseph Lefebvre, after completing the painting he travelled for several months. When he returned his subject had tragically died by her own hand. "She was a girl of more refinement and elevation of sentiment than is usually to be found among persons of her position," he said, "and driven to despair, the poor child poisoned herself by washing phosphorus from friction matches and then swallowing the decoction."

Could it be the woman at the top of the stairs and the one at the bottom have more in common than the lovelorn drinkers suspect?

A PIECE OF AMERICAN HISTORY

The three-bedroom farmhouse in Villisca, Iowa is beautiful. Like a doll's house it has white clapboard walls, a gabled roof and a porch perfect for a rocking chair. Only the sign in the front garden gives one pause: "The Villisca Ax Murder House, June 10 1912".

Darwin and Martha Linn bought the house in 1994 and planned to turn it into a museum, a look into how life was in the early twentieth century. But there was something about the house which the estate agent may have forgotten to mention.

On the evening of June 9 1912, the Moore family, Josiah and Sarah and their four children, Herman (11), Mary (10), Arthur (7) and Paul (5), had been joined for the night by two of Mary's friends, sisters Ina Mae (8) and Lena Stillinger (12). They spent the evening at their local church at a Children's Day service.

The next day a neighbour, Mary Peckham, became concerned when she noticed the Moores had not come out to do their morning chores. She fetched Josiah's brother Ross and tried knocking on the farmhouse door. No one answered so they unlocked the door and went inside.

There they found the two Stillinger girls dead in the guest bedroom. They had been bludgeoned to death. In the other bedrooms lay Josiah and Sarah and all the Moore children, who had also been murdered the same way. The murder weapon, Josiah's axe, was found in the guest room, drenched in the blood of its six victims. Next to it was placed a slab of bacon from the icebox. In the basement they found cigarette butts which they guessed were left behind by the killer as they patiently waited for the family to go to sleep. All the mirrors in the house had been covered, as had the faces of the victims. A bowl of bloody water suggested that the killer had washed their hands afterwards.

There were many suspects who had been in the town that night for the popular Children's Day service. They included the Reverend George Kelly, who was committed to a mental hospital two years later, and Paul Mueller, a German immigrant and, it would be discovered later, a serial killer whose 59 victims all lived near railway tracks, and whose modus operandi was that of the Moores' killer. Both were questioned by police but no one was ever found guilty.

Having discovered the house's murky history, Darwin and Martha Linn decided not to open a museum. Since 1912 many unusual things have purportedly happened at the house. There have been reports of the sounds of giggling and screaming, and of a strange fog that moves through the house when a train passes in the night. Some visitors have seemingly become possessed. Most of the enquiries the Linns were getting at their museum were from paranormal investigators, eager to explore the house and on occasion sleep in the rooms where the murders took place.

And so the Mueller Villisca Ax Murder House became a hotel of sorts, where anyone can stay (for a small fee). Martha will hand you the key and leave you to it. Maybe you'll get a good night's sleep. Or maybe you'll end up more like Robert Steven Laursen Jr. of Wisconsin who stayed there with friends in 2014, for a "recreational paranormal investigation". At 12.45 a.m., in the very room in which the Moores were bludgeoned to death, Laursen stabbed himself in the chest, almost bleeding to death. He's never spoken about why he did it. Or perhaps he has no words.

Booking available online, or give them a call.

THE LAST BUS

Ghosts are everywhere in China, according to folk belief. First of all, there are the ancestor spirits which supposedly remain with their families for centuries after their physical bodies have died. In traditional Chinese religion, everyone has two souls: the *han*, which ascends into heaven when a person dies, and the *po*, which stays on Earth. A family must pay respect to the *han* spirit through rituals – woe betide anyone who does not! These spirits become godly beings who can play with the destinies of those on Earth. If you want good luck in this world, you had better pay tribute to these beings in the next world.

If you fail to conduct the proper rituals when your ancestor dies, their spirit may join the hungry ghosts who are released from heaven on the fifteenth day of the seventh month of the Chinese calendar, and who take part in the Hungry Ghost Festival. Roaming the Earth, they seek the food which was denied them during the death rituals. You can tell a hungry ghost as they reputedly have a long thin neck, showing that they were underfed by their wicked family. If you think a hungry ghost is coming, you had better have a meal ready and offer prayers. Some people burn banknotes – and even cars and television sets – to punish themselves and hopefully appease the ghost. If it works, you will have a year's grace before the hungry ghost comes looking again.

Ghosts can be inventive, and they don't always feel the need to roam in a spooky fashion. They might travel in a more conventional way...

Most of us know what it is like to take the last bus home. It is dark outside, the bus never seems to arrive, and when it does it is almost empty. So in 1995, when a young man stepped onto the last bus to Xiang-Shan, a place known as Fragrant Hills, he might have been relieved to see the bus, but may well have been nervous as it was so empty. No one was on it apart from the driver and conductor, and a very old woman.

Soon after, the driver was hailed by two men on the side of the road. Although they were not at a bus stop, the driver took pity on them and let them on. Strangely, they were dressed in robes from around 300 years ago. They were carrying a third man with long messy hair. They all sat down. The young man noticed how white their faces were.

The young man heard a scream. The old woman was standing above him. "You've stolen my wallet," she screamed. The young man said he had not. The old woman insisted, grabbing the conductor and repeating the accusation. The young man again denied it. The old woman demanded the bus be stopped so she could take the young man to the police station. "Just here!" she screamed. "There is one just here!" The driver stopped and the young man reluctantly got off.

There was no police station. The young man became angry at the old woman. "Why did you do that?" the man demanded. The old woman looked at him tenderly. "You see," she said, "when those two men got on, the wind lifted their robes a little

– and they had no legs. They were not men, my child, they were ghosts. I had to get us both off the bus."

The next day the bus was reported missing. It was found four miles before its destination, and inside were the corpses of the driver, the conductor and an unknown man with long messy hair...

DO NOT GO GENTLE

The Chelsea Hotel in New York is famous for many reasons. Many of the great, the good and the not-so-good have stayed there. Leonard Cohen famously wrote a song about a night there with Janis Joplin, while in a less happy rendezvous, Sid Vicious stabbed his girlfriend Nancy Spungen there. Science fiction author Arthur C. Clarke and film director Stanley Kubrick wrote the screenplay for *2001: A Space Odyssey* there, and the poet Allen Ginsberg hung out at the Chelsea for his countercultural "happenings" – experimental performances of art, music and poetry.

The ghost of another poet apparently visited a horrified guest there in 2009. The guest, identified only as "Anna", had already endured a couple of sleepless nights at the hotel, hearing footsteps and murmuring voices. But it was on the third night that she said she woke to a terrible sight. There, floating in front of her mirror, was the bug-eyed spirit of the twentieth-century Welsh bard Dylan Thomas.

"I suddenly looked up and right in front of the bedroom mirror, I saw a head in mid-air," Anna is recorded to have said. "The head seemed to grimace at me, and I will never forget the eyes staring me down, almost bug-eyed." She also described the head as wearing theatrical face paint and lipstick, and having "ear-length tightly coiled black hair".

Even in her bewildered state, Anna was sure she knew the face. Then it suddenly dawned on her who it was and why he was there.

Dylan Thomas stayed at the Chelsea Hotel in 1953 during the New York leg – or New York legless – part of his literary tour of the US. According to legend, on the night of 9 November the infamously hard-drinking poet downed 18 neat whiskies at the White Horse Tavern in Greenwich Village, before stumbling back to his room. By the morning, he was no longer with us.

Thomas' ghost has some form in this area. The White Horse Tavern itself is said to be visited by him sometimes, to the extent that patrons raised a petition to block a planned renovation of the bar in case he never came back. The renovations took place, and apparently the ghost returned – nothing gets between a poet and a drink!

And so the man who wrote one of the greatest of all poems about death, "Do Not Go Gentle Into That Good Night", seems to have taken his own advice, although a spokesman for the hotel scoffed at Anna's claims.

"The ghost of Dylan Thomas does not haunt Room 114 of the Chelsea Hotel," he said. "It haunts 205 where he was staying."

DOMESTIC ISSUES

When most of the world was in lockdown in 2020, perhaps the happiest creatures on Earth were dogs, who had their human companions around them all day every day. But what about ghosts? It has never really been clear if ghosts enjoy human company. Some of their more malicious actions suggest not, but perhaps they have no other way of showing their affection than by rattling chains, lifting toilet seats or making blood run down walls.

All we know is that during lockdown paranormal researchers recorded a large spike in the number of people who reported unexplained phenomena in their homes. Things turning up in places they hadn't been left. Disembodied voices. Electronic devices turning off and on. Being touched, when there were no visible hands there to touch them.

Perhaps there are rational explanations for this. Even someone like John E. L. Tenney, a paranormal researcher himself, is more than happy to acknowledge that people can confuse the pops and clicks of a central heating system with supernatural sounds. And perhaps with everyone stuck at home due to the pandemic, we all became more anxiously sensitive to our surroundings.

But – if you were an unfriendly ghost, wouldn't a lot

of nervous people locked in houses present plenty of opportunities for mischief? Or if you were a ghost used to having the house to yourself all day, might you not wish to make your dissatisfaction at the new circumstances known, any way you could?

According to the *New York Times*, one couple in Nashville ended up having to share their house with a spirit they called Matthew – a "good biblical name", they said. If giving Matthew a name was supposed to appease him, it did not work. Every night, Matthew would take to running up and down the stairs "very clearly to get our attention", said the couple. It was too loud to be the family cat, who no doubt had other ways to express its dissatisfaction at no longer having the house to itself.

And if sleep deprivation wasn't bad enough, Matthew had other tricks up his sleeve. When one of the couple was showering, they would be hit by a blast of cold water. Staggering out, they found the same thing each time: the hot water had been turned off at the wall. While this is not the worst thing a ghost can do, no one who has suddenly been hit by a blast of cold water in the shower like this could call Matthew's actions civil.

But for every Matthew causing domestic mayhem, there may be a ghost who prefers to be helpful. One couple in Queens, New York reported that a source of huge tension between them had been night-time possession of their shared blanket. Many a tug of war happened between the hours of lights out and morning. Then one night, Kerry was in bed waiting for Alexandra, his wife. He felt the blanket move, but instead of being pulled to the other side of the bed, it was being straightened and spread evenly. He rolled over to thank Alexandra for her concern. She did not respond. She was in the bathroom.

A few weeks later he saw a small Asian woman in his kitchen wearing green scrubs, who he said was glowing and who disappeared when he turned on the light. Could this apparition have been the helpful blanket-straightener and the reason why Kerry and Alexandra are now sleeping so well?

THE WHITE LADY OF BOHEMIA

Standing on a promontory carved out on three sides by the river Vltava, Rožmberk Castle is one of the oldest castles in Bohemia in the Czech Republic. First mentioned in 1253, it was the home of the Rožmberk family, one of the most powerful and prosperous Czech families in their day. Visitors to the castle can see the ornate music room, the message "love disappears, colours fade" carved into the wall in the seventeenth century by Spanish soldiers and a portrait of the woman whose tragic fate continues to haunt the castle – Perchta of Rožmberk, daughter of the all-powerful King Oldrich II, and the famous White Lady of Bohemia.

In 1449, Oldrich married his daughter off to Jan of Liechtenstein. It was an abusive relationship about which Perchta was profoundly unhappy. She wrote many letters pleading with her father and brother to rescue her. Ninety-two of the messages survive, showing how lonely and desperate Perchta was. When her father failed to pay her dowry, her husband grew crueller, with his mother and sister joining in the persecution. "Take me away from these evil people and you will merit praise, as if you released a soul from Purgatory,"

Perchta wrote to her brothers, to no avail.

All of her brothers died before her, as did all of her children. Her life was spent burying her relatives. Jan's brutality was such that when on his death bed he asked her to forgive him his crimes to ensure he would go to heaven, she refused him, cursing him instead. Even after his passing his mother and sister continued to taunt Perchta. She sincerely hoped death would bring her peace.

But when she died in 1476 her spirit, legend has it, remained as restless and tormented as when she was alive. She became the famous White Lady of Bohemia, fated to haunt her family's old estates. Whenever something important was about to happen to the Rožmberks, she appeared, holding a pair of gloves in her hands. White gloves meant something joyous, black gloves disaster. Over time the black gloves appeared more and more frequently.

But Perchta gave her family and nation one final act of generosity. When Petr Vok, the last of the Rožmberks, was a baby, the nurse who was supposed to be caring for him fell asleep. The baby fell ill and came close to death. The White Lady of Bohemia allegedly cared for young Petr, curing his fever and waking the nurse, whom she then chastened for her carelessness, before disappearing. When Bohemia was threatened in 1611 by Germany, Petr melted down all of the Rožmberk treasure, turning it into coins to pay off the marauding army. Supposedly at his shoulder was a lady in white, holding a pair of white gloves.

Some say that this was her last appearance, that the White Lady of Bohemia departed this Earth when her family did. But others think she still haunts the castles associated with her unhappy life. One theory holds that she is the goddess Perchta, who in winter rewards good children with silver. Bad ones she disembowels, replacing their organs with rocks.

On the portrait of Perchta, the White Lady of Bohemia, there is a weird caption in the "Enochian script" invented by the sixteenth-century English occultists John Dee and Edward Kelley. No one knows how it got there or what it says. They say whoever deciphers it will win Perchta her freedom. No one has thus far.

THE OLDEST DRAWING OF A GHOST?

The tablet is small enough to fit in your hand. At first glance there seems only to be writing, but closer inspection reveals two figures carved into it, one of a man and the other…

When the curator of the British Museum's Middle Eastern Department first examined the 3,500-year-old stone tablet from Babylon in 2021, he was intrigued. The second figure, although still humanoid, seemed very different from the normal figures of that era. It looked like a ghost.

Not only that, the writing on the tablet turned out to be a set of instructions on how to get rid of ghosts. First, you need to make two figurines, one of a man, one of a woman. Then make some beer (it is not clear whether this is part of the exorcism, or whether it's just a good thing to steady the nerves and get you through what may be a long night).

Wait until sunrise and then speak ritual words calling to the god Shamash (presumably don't have too much of the beer before doing this), who is responsible for taking ghosts down to the Underworld. It seems the idea was that Shamash would catch the ghost in the figurine of the right sex, and off they would go. (A section is broken off at this point, but presumably it says something like "Finish the beer.")

But it seems that some things never change when it comes to ghosts. The final line of the tablet speaks down the 3,500 years to anyone who fears ghosts. "Don't," it says, "look behind you!"

DONALD

Not all ghost stories happen in castles. Sometimes they occur in the most ordinary houses, such as number 63, Wycliffe Road, Battersea, South London, England. In this unassuming, semi-detached house a poltergeist made itself at home and became so famous it was discussed in Parliament.

As many a ghost hunter will tell you, a poltergeist is a specific sort of ghost. The word comes from the German *"poltern"* (noisy) and *"geist"* (ghost). These "noisy ghosts" tend to stay in one location and make themselves known. Objects fly around, wardrobes fall down and there is often a foul smell.

None of which the Hitchings family was aware of in 1956 when they moved into number 63. Dad Wally was a train driver, his wheelchair-bound wife Kitty a former office clerk and their 15-year-old daughter Shirley was at school.

It started with a key, which Shirley found on her pillow one afternoon. She gave it to her father, who tried every lock in the house. It fitted none. He placed it on the mantlepiece and thought no more of it.

At 2 a.m. that night the whole family was woken by tremendous banging inside the walls and floorboards, so loud that neighbours complained. The next night, the same banging. The police and the fire brigade investigated. They found nothing.

Also, the key had disappeared.

Soon after, objects including clocks, pots and pans flew through the air seemingly of their own volition. Slippers walked around rooms without their owners. At times the activities became so violent that entire rooms would end up trashed. The family piano would start to play of its own accord.

Worse was to follow. One night Wally and Kitty heard Shirley screaming. They ran to her room to find her bedsheets apparently being dragged from her. A tug of war ensued as the family and whatever it was battled over the teenager. Once they got her back in bed they were even more shocked when her body began levitating several inches above the bed, so they claimed. These events were later to be immortalized in Tobe Hooper's 1982 film *Poltergeist*. Shirley said, "We were scared out of our wits. I thought, 'This is the end. We're all going to die.'"

By February the story of 63 Wycliffe Road was in the national press. It was then that "ghost hunter" Harold "Chib" Chibbett became involved. Deciding that this was a poltergeist, whose victims tend to be teenage girls, Chib suggested an exorcism for Shirley. In desperation the Hitchings family agreed, only for the exorcism to be stopped by the police, who were suspicious that Chib was practising black magic. In Parliament, the family's local MP called on the police to apologize for meddling.

By now the family had named the visitor "Donald" after Donald Duck for its bad temper. Chib suggested trying to make contact, and used letter cards to help Donald communicate. Donald claimed to be French and to be scared. There were messages such as "Shirley, I come." He started making demands of the terrified teenager, asking her to wear her hair a certain way and threatening to start fires if she didn't.

HAUNTINGS

Allegedly, Donald continued to stalk Shirley even after she left 63 Wycliffe Road. He would send her messages on notepads. Then in 1968, he wrote a final note which said he was leaving. He kept the promise. "My mum went into mourning," Shirley says. "She'd got to think of Donald like a son. But Dad and I were delighted."

The house was demolished in the late 1960s. A new house stands on the spot. It looks very unassuming.

THE WHISTLER

It begins with the sound of whistling.

It is always the same tune, running through C, D, E, F and then lowering to G, A and B in that order. If you hear it nearby, then you are safe. It is only when it is in the distance that you can be sure it is El Silbón, The Whistler, who is coming for you.

In Venezuela and Colombia there are various theories about why El Silbón seeks revenge. He might be a farmer's son who killed his father for womanizing, and who was in turn tortured and killed by his grandfather. Or perhaps his father's drunkenness led El Silbón to kill him, and for the grandfather to take revenge against his grandson. The revenge includes being set upon by rabid dogs and being forced to carry his father's bones for eternity.

In another story, El Silbón was simply a spoiled young boy who killed his father after his father failed to serve his favourite dinner. He presented his father's entrails to his mother, who cooked and ate them with her son. When she found out what he had done, she cursed him to wander the Earth forever.

Certainly, it is drunks and womanizers who should worry most about El Silbón. He is most often heard in Los Llanos, the tropical plains east of the Andes where Venezuela and Colombia meet. He is, they say, a tall thin man with a straw hat, with chunks of flesh hanging from him. He is often in Los Llanos during the harsh summer drought – when the Orinoco River dries up and a lonely man's thoughts turn to alcohol and to women other than those they have left behind. He is said to tear womanizers to pieces and to suck the alcohol out through the navels of drunks as they die.

But sometimes he likes to branch out. El Silbón has also been known to visit families and sit in their doorways to count his bones. If anyone in the family fails to listen attentively to him, the whole family will die. Therefore, one should never utter his name during the nights, lest he is summoned. Some say it is his loneliness that drives him on, and if no one will pay him the small mercy of listening to him count, then he will repay their cruelty as he repaid his father's.

If you are lucky, when you encounter him you may save yourself by producing a chilli, which reminds him of his crime, or a whip, which reminds him of his punishment. They say the barking of a dog may be one way of keeping him at bay. It is the only thing on Earth El Silbón fears. It has also been said that saying the Lord's Prayer may scare him off, but none have survived to confirm this.

And if you are killed by El Silbón? Then your bones are his, to be added to the sack in which he keeps his father's. You will be cursed to walk the Earth in pursuit of The Whistler, for no one can pass to the other side without their bones.

They say the number of drunks and womanizers in the plains east of the Andes has fallen in recent years. Maybe El Silbón's good work is having an effect. It might mean he has to labour further afield, perhaps near where you are? But as long as you don't drink too much and are always faithful, you should be safe, shouldn't you?

THE KASHA

"She's trying to kill my children! She's trying to kill my children!"

When police in Hawai'i took this call in 1941, they may have had other things on their minds. Only a few months earlier the Japanese had attacked nearby Pearl Harbor. But the terrified voice of the woman shook them out of any reverie, and they dashed to the house in Kaimuki. When they arrived they found a woman, her three daughters and one son being tossed around and levitated. They could only watch on in horror – whoever or whatever was doing this to them was invisible.

This was not the last incident that would happen at the house. In the following years a young boy would smell what he swore was the odour of a ghost, enraging it so it attacked the boy's family and police officers. Thirty years after the first incident, three girls staying in the house heard strange noises and contacted the police. An officer who attended offered to follow their car as they left. As they pulled into a car park he saw one of the girls trying to fight off… something. He ran to the car, reached in and, he said, "a big, strong calloused hand that could not possibly belong to a teenaged girl grabbed my arm and twisted it". The girl fell down, grabbing her own throat. She was barely alive.

There are many theories as to the identity of the attacker, but those in the region will tell you there is no doubt it is the kasha, a shape-shifting spirit from Japan. Often assuming the form of a troll or a humanoid cat-demon with a burning tail, it roams the world stealing the corpses of the recently dead, who are not yet buried but have led sinful lives. The kasha drags them down to hell. In another version of the story, the kasha feeds on the corpses of the dead, sinful or otherwise. And its appetite is insatiable.

Why would the kasha choose this spot? It seems that the house had a violent past even before that day in 1941. They say that, a few years earlier, the father of the family that used to live there killed his wife, son and daughter. The wife and son's bodies were found buried in the back garden. But the daughter was never located. Could it be that the kasha came for the girl? Was it something sinful she had done that enraged the father? Or is she still down there somewhere, and the kasha is looking for her, furious about having missed out on a ripe corpse?

So frequent were the attacks that in 2016 the house was torn down and rituals performed to make the kasha go away. Japanese holy men have long used ways to trick the kasha and keep the dead safe from his avarice. Chanting or playing a *myobachi* (traditional Japanese instrument) will do it. Or filling coffins with stones to fool the kasha into digging up the wrong grave.

But perhaps the kasha is learning, or the tricks aimed at stopping it are losing their power, for residents of the new condominium built on the spot of the Kasha House of Kaimuki have reported strange goings-on. Could it be the search for the missing daughter continues? And that the kasha will not rest until she is found?

HAUNTINGS

Ghost or demon – whether cat- or troll-shaped – does it matter as a calloused hand grabs your arms and twists?

GOOD LADY ISOBEL

Ghosts tend to get a pretty bad rap. They are either scaring people or killing people or scaring people and then killing people. On and on it goes.

But if you ever find yourself waking to a strange presence at Ballygally Castle in County Antrim, Northern Ireland, you will be in for a pleasant surprise.

It is haunted by the ghost of Lady Isobel Shaw, who is said to be the friendliest ghost this side of Caspar. She may be found either wandering the corridors of the castle or making a warm green mist descend, which is known to feel quite lovely.

It is said that 400 years ago her husband, Lord Shaw, was so angry at her for not producing a male heir that he locked her in the top of the castle to die. She fell to her death trying to escape. Or, in another version, he threw her off the tower himself in his anger.

Why this has led to her being quite so friendly nobody knows. Perhaps she is just a very nice person, who is happy to get up, dust herself off and get on with things, no matter what has happened to her – being thrown off the tower of a castle by an angry husband included.

One thing: Lord Shaw seems to have gone missing shortly after her death, possibly in a terrible accident... All's well that ends well.

THE BLACK-EYED CHILDREN

We all know the scene. We are watching a movie with a ghost in it. Already scared, we dread the moment when the unquiet spirit is revealed to us. Will it be the lady who died in the house a century ago? Or the old farmer who perished in the barn one stormy night? No, it's worse – it's a child!

There is something especially creepy about child ghosts. England has its share of them, such as the Radiant Boy who haunts the northern county of Lincolnshire, sneaking up on unsuspecting farmers with his wide eyes and glowing face. Sometimes he is on horseback, sometimes he just levitates. He has also been known to hang out at Corby Castle, the ancestral home of Catherine Howard, fifth wife of Henry VIII. The king had her beheaded in 1541 for adultery. Perhaps the Radiant Boy came to a similarly sticky end?

But it is the United States which seems home to the most ghost children. Some seem good-natured, like the Ghost Boy of Clinton Road in New Jersey, who spends his time under a bridge over a notorious hairpin bend. Some say he fell from the bridge after being dared to balance on the edge by friends; others say he was hit by a car while bending to pick up a quarter. Whichever is true, it is well known in the area that, if you throw a coin from the bridge at midnight, he will throw it back to you. Go there and you'll see lots of coins in the river. Perhaps these people did it at the wrong moment, a second too early or a second too late. What we can never see is the coins which were returned...

In Huntsville, Alabama, not only is the Dead Children's Playground in the grounds of a cemetery, but it is claustrophobically surrounded on three sides by rocks and trees. People have reported swings moving back and forth in still weather, the sound of children laughing when there is no one there. Some even report seeing little kids climbing on the jungle gym in the dead of night, with no parents watching.

But the locals obviously like it that way. When the playground was razed to the ground in 2007 to make more room for burials, they rebuilt it. They must know how angry and bored kids get when they can't spend time... outside.

But if these are ghost children you might like to be around, what about the Black-eyed Children? First encountered in 2016, these little mites are not the sort of company you want to keep. With pale skin and blacked-out eyes, they are usually encountered hitchhiking, begging or on your doorstep asking to use the bathroom.

They usually ask for help, but that's just a ploy to infiltrate your house or your car. One family in Vermont opened their door to two children, a boy and a girl. "Our parents will be here soon, may we come in?" asked the boy. Once inside they went to the bathroom. The wife said to her husband, "Did you see their eyes? Black as a starless night." Moments later the husband's nose started bleeding. The lights went out. And the children disappeared.

Since then, all four of the couple's cats have gone missing, the nosebleeds have continued and the man has been diagnosed with aggressive skin cancer.

Some say the Black-eyed Children are not ghosts, but the Devil himself.

THE IMAGINARY FRIEND

Did you have an imaginary friend when you were growing up? Someone you could play with when you were by yourself. Someone you could tell your secrets to? A best friend forever, until you grew a little older? Something you grew out of, right? A child psychiatrist would see that as perfectly normal behaviour, even healthy. And yet...

When Kellie's daughter Madison was first able to walk, she got her first imaginary friend. Friends, in fact, because as she later explained, they always came in pairs. By the age of three, this little girl from Macon, Georgia had at least six friends: Dana and Steve, Froga and Kinga, and Boyfriend and Girlfriend. They would play together all day, Madison chatting brightly to them.

Soon after her third birthday, Madison announced she had a new friend, Kellum. For the first time it was a friend, singular, which made Kellie curious. She asked Madison to tell her about Kellum. He was a boy, Madison said. He always dressed in "outside clothes". He liked Madison to make Play-Doh sandwiches and build towers out of blocks they could knock down.

Oh, and he was in his forties, and had a beard.

When Kellie first heard this she was understandably worried.

But Madison's friends had come and gone before. She was sure "Kellum" would be the same. And then Madison told her about the song, "Daisy Bell", which features the lyric "Daisy, tell me your answer do…"

Kellum had taught it to her, Madison said. She knew all the words and the melody of this song, which Kellie had never played for her. Kellie asked Madison's babysitter if she had taught it to her. She said no. Madison told her mother again, Kellum taught it to her. "He sings it to his baby girl."

Then things started to go bad. Madison grew sleepy and irritable. She told Kellie that Kellum had kept her up all night. He always wanted to play. He would bang things if she tried to sleep, or yell at her if she wanted to stop the games. Listening to a baby monitor in the night, Kellie heard Madison talking to Kellum. "Leave me alone, Kellum, I don't want to play with you anymore."

Also, Madison said, Kellum was changing. His face was dirty. He was getting skinnier, and his eyes were sunken. She didn't like him anymore. She was scared of him now.

Then one night Kellie woke to the sound of Madison screaming. She ran to the little girl's bedroom. The curtains were billowing, even though the windows were shut. Madison was still screaming, so Kellie grabbed her and ran from the house. Not knowing what else to do, she called her father-in-law, who was a God-fearing pastor. He ran to the house, telling them to stay away. Two hours later he told them they could return. He'd used anointing oil to draw crosses all over the house. And Kellie and Madison could sense straight away that Kellum was gone.

A little while later, Kellie was doing some research about her area. She saw that a neighbouring house had been bought in 1941 by a man named Callum Beasley. Callum had five children, four of whom had grown to adulthood. But the fifth was a little girl named Madeline. She had died when she was three, the same age Madison was when Kellum arrived, singing to his baby girl.

Madison never had another imaginary friend. But don't forget, having one is not so strange.

ON FILM

The camera never lies, they say. There are some people who would have you believe that the ghostly figure coming down the stairs in a photograph is the result of light on the lens, as with the famous Brown Lady captured on film at Raynham Hall in Norfolk. Or that any blurred figure can look like a ghost with enough imagination. Some early ghost photographers later admitted they used double exposure to fool the public. And nowadays any digital photo can be manipulated.

But in 2015, when 12-year-old Holly Hampsheir pulled out her iPhone to take a picture of her cousin Brook at the sixteenth-century stately home Hampton Court, neither of them knew that they would soon be making headlines. In fact, Holly took several more pictures one after the other, as teenagers do. All except one show just Brook, looking at the magnificent King's Palace paintings. All except one.

"I was totally freaked out," said Holly when she saw the picture she had taken. There, standing behind Brook, was a tall woman, dressed in blue, with long flowing brown hair, as stately as the house itself. This was no case of light on the lens, wishful thinking or double exposure. Nothing was manipulated – the girls saw the picture moments after they took it and immediately showed Brook's mother. Experts are baffled and can offer no explanation.

But for those who know their ghosts, there is only one answer. This is the famous Grey Lady whose sullen visage has supposedly haunted Hampton Court for centuries. She is widely believed to be the spectre of Dame Sybil Penn, who died of smallpox in the house in 1562 after nursing Queen Elizabeth I through the disease. She first appeared in 1829 when Dame Sybil's tomb was moved. Legend has it that a spinning wheel can be heard turning in the night, and subsequent investigations found a secret chamber in the palace – containing an antique spinning wheel.

If she is still at the palace, she is in good company. The ghosts of two of Henry VIII's wives have been sighted. Jane Seymour, who died after giving birth, haunts the Silverwick stairs leading to the room where she died. Catherine Howard, who Henry had beheaded, runs through the palace, screaming for mercy as she did the day she was killed.

And while not everyone can be as lucky as Holly and capture a full-size ghost on camera, paranormal investigators now use film to identify the presence of ghosts even where no one has reported disturbances, by capturing ghost orbs. These are small balls of light which are invisible to the naked eye but show up in videos and photographs.

Believed to be manifestations of energy trapped on Earth after death, ghost orbs move rapidly from room to room. They come in many colours, and experienced investigators can work out the type of ghost from the colour of the orb – white ones, while positive, may show a ghost stuck on a plane of being they don't belong to. Red and orange orbs are protective ghosts, giving off a warm glow to show they will help. One should also be happy to encounter blue orbs, for they may have healing powers, as can green orbs, although these may be spirits who have never lived on Earth, such as dead infants.

But if you happen to encounter a black orb, get away quick as you can. Evil dwells in them. Not that you can see them. You'd have no idea if one was in the room with you right now, unless you anger it...

WILL THE BLACKSMITH

Once upon a time there was a blacksmith named Will. A drunk, philanderer and troublemaker, when Will died and went to heaven St Peter decided to send him back to Earth for another shot at being good. But Will was just as bad during his second life, possibly worse. This time St Peter showed no mercy. Will was cursed to walk the Earth for eternity.

The Devil, seeing a kindred spirit, gave Will a lump of coal to keep him warm. Will, who could out-devil the Devil, had other plans. He would place the coal in a torch and use its light to lure travellers to their death. From that day forth, many a lonely wanderer would encounter a strange glow on the horizon, a wispy light they felt compelled to follow. And many a wanderer would find themselves falling off precipices, into ravines and sometimes even off the edge of the world.

Thus has Will-o'-the-wisp entertained himself for many centuries. He, too, is a traveller, apparently sighted all over the world. In some regions of England and Ireland he goes by the name of Jack-o'-Lantern, the ghost of the notorious drunk Stingy Jack. Down south in Devon and Cornwall he is associated with pixie-light, which mischievously blows out candles and makes kissing noises to fool parents into thinking their children are up to no good. Off the south coast in Guernsey he is Faeu Bolanger, or the rolling fire, a lost soul who wishes only that you join him in death.

In Argentina, he is Luz Mala, the evil light, and it is said that the ghostly light is the souls of the dead, crying in pain. In Brazil he takes the form of a serpent called Boi-tata. Surviving a great deluge, Boi-tata left his dry cave and ate the eyes of all the dead creatures, and it is they that gave him his fiery gaze.

In Sweden he is the soul of an unbaptized man, trying to lead travellers to water so they can immerse him in God's spirit. The Bengalis see him in the marshes, luring fishermen too far from land to join the dead, the fishermens' spirits adding to the radiance of the light. Further south in Australia this light is called Min Min Bio, and it is possible that not all of those early explorers became lost in the outback due to deficient maps. Perhaps they were following a wisp on its way?

So if you see Will, it might be best to turn away. Although some, such as those in Finland, Denmark and Estonia, believe that the glow of his torch shows the location of buried treasure. For the Finns it is best to look on St John's Day, as on no other day will the dead allow access to the treasure. If you are Estonian, no such restrictions apply, and you should hasten to where Will has his lantern straight away.

And if you are Irish, well, it's not just at the end of rainbows you might find treasure. The glow of Will's torch might lead you to discover the buried treasure beside the banks of the river Lagan in Northern Ireland. A zealous apparition of a monk warns travellers it is sacrilegious to seek the treasure, as this was the spot where there was to be a church built "to match the magnificence of St Peter's in Rome".

Perhaps Will the Blacksmith still seeks victory over St Peter?

THE IROQUOIS
THEATRE, CHICAGO

It was during a matinee performance of *Mr. Blue Beard* – the story of a man who kills all his wives, showing each new one the corpses of the earlier ones – that the fire broke out. On 30 December 1903, the Iroquois Theatre had only been open for six weeks, but that day it was full to the rafters with 1,724 patrons. Despite the grisly story, the play had been made into a children's comedy by having the wives all come back at the end and dance. Those in the theatre that night would not be so lucky.

According to the superstitious, the theatrical world has long been haunted by the ghosts of actors stabbed by jealous rivals who come back to terrorize the place they died, of actresses poisoned by understudies who coveted their fame returning to weep in dressing rooms. But on that day in 1903, the Iroquois became perhaps the most haunted theatre in the world – some 602 perished in the conflagration.

Of these, only about 100 could be identified, the rest were so badly burned as to be unrecognizable. It was only by checking "trinkets and burned scraps of wearing apparel" that the bodies of hundreds would be "made known to their families". Many of the dead were children, dressed in their finery.

HAUNTINGS

The first act had been incident free. Then during the second act, at 3.20 p.m., while ballerinas danced to a song called "Let Us Swear It by the Pale Moonlight", a bang was heard. One of the stage lights exploded. The actors stopped and called for calm – costing a million pounds, this was the most state-of-the-art theatre yet and totally fireproof.

People were exhorted to exit calmly. There were, after all, 30 fire exits, more than in any other theatre in the world. However, there were no lights showing the exits. The exit doors had also been bolted, so no one could sneak in for free.

Ten minutes later almost half the patrons were dead, some burned, some from leaping out of windows. On one thing the owners were right: the building didn't collapse.

It was, however, torn down and rebuilt in 1926 as the Oriental Theatre, now called the Nederlander. But this does not seem to have appeased the ghosts of the Iroquois. Actors and stagehands report seeing shadowy figures in the balconies as they rehearse. Others claim to have seen strange figures in period dress in stairwells or moving down corridors. One singer who was being hoisted on ropes in a performance of *Wicked* suspected she was being stared at from the gallery as she was swung around the stage.

And then there are the children. Young voices being heard in empty rooms, sometimes giggling, sometimes crying, and sometimes, worst of all, screaming. Still dressed in their finery, no doubt, perhaps they are waiting for the pretty ballerinas to resume their act. Some actors have refused to work in the theatre as the presence of the children remains so strong.

And creepiest of all is the alley beside the theatre that legions of the ill-fated theatre-goers tried to escape down, or where they jumped to their deaths. It has been renamed Death Alley.

Even on the warmest days there is a cold breeze going down it, and people report feeling hands on their shoulders or pulling on their coats. You may even hear someone whisper your name. They are almost certainly asking, over a hundred years too late, if you happen to know the way to the exit.

THE GHOUL

Apparition, phantom, poltergeist, spectre, spirit, wraith. There are many ways to refer to a ghost. Whether the ghosts care or not is, of course, not known, but one can speculate.

When it comes to ghouls, though, there does seem to be an important distinction. The name comes from the Arabic word *"ghūl"*, which means "to seize", and it seems that the average ghoul will take any opportunity not only to seize but to devour.

Believed in Arabic folklore to inhabit cemeteries, where they feed on both corpses and mourners, they also seem to be prevalent in desert areas, where they slay victims they have tempted into the wilderness. Particularly tasty are children. Sometimes the ghoul may even take on the form of the victim it has just devoured in order to feast on their friends and family. Always be wary if one of your desert party leaves the fold and does not return for some time. To be on the safe side, it might be best to kill them before they have a chance to kill you.

The ghoul you really don't want to meet is Mother Ghoul, who turns up in too many stories to be imaginary. She will tempt you into her clutches, particularly if you are a man, and you will never be seen again. When men in Arab countries leave their wives and disappear, this is almost certainly what has happened.

So if, after a while, he comes back, don't let him in until you're sure it's not actually Mother Ghoul in disguise, hungry for more victims.

HANAKO-SAN AND KASHIMA REIKO

She has a bobbed haircut and wears a little red dress. If you want to summon her, you go to the third stall of the girls' school toilet (usually on the third floor) and knock three times. You should also call her name – "Hanako-san" – three times. "Hanako-san, Hanako-san, Hanako-san." If she is there, she will reply, "Yes, I am." If you are lucky, all that will happen next is that you will see a bloody hand. If you are really unlucky, the hand will grab you and pull you into the stall, and then into the toilet, which will lead you down to hell.

No one is entirely sure how Hanako-san got there. Some say she was murdered in a school toilet, others that she committed suicide there. Most often it is said she was in the toilet during World War Two playing hide-and-seek when there was an Allied air raid. Torn between not being found and running for cover, she was killed by a bomb.

Allegedly, her spirit now haunts all girls' school toilets. Some believe she just wants to be friends, but how does that explain that she sometimes is accompanied by a three-headed lizard that will eat you for invading her privacy?

Japanese children are told not to disturb Hanako-san – girls should always avoid the third stall, while boys should not become overly curious. It is also a good idea not to dally too long on the toilet – while Hanako-san seems trapped in one stall, nothing can be guaranteed.

And yet the temptation to knock three times and say, "Hanako-san, Hanako-san, Hanako-san" can be almost overwhelming. We all know what little children are like. It only takes a few of them egging each other on and disasters can happen. It is best, then, to stay away from little girls who might dare you to knock.

Especially as you might not just meet Hanako-san. You might also encounter Kashima Reiko, who is also thought to haunt toilet stalls. She is one of the Teke Teke, the ghosts of little girls who have fallen on the train line. The lower halves of their bodies are gone, and so they travel on their hands, dragging their bodies along the ground, which makes a distinctive "teke teke" sound.

Kashima died when her legs were severed from her body by a moving train. She is believed to haunt bathroom stalls asking anyone who comes in where her legs are. If she does not accept the response, she will exact revenge by removing their legs, some say by tearing them off, others by cutting them from the body. Other stories have her carrying a scythe in order to do this, and say that she enjoys seeing the bodies of her prey mirror her own in stopping halfway down – although her victims will not survive to make the "teke teke" sound.

The answer you should give to her question is "On the Meishin Expressway", which is where she is said to have met her grisly fate. Alternatively, you can say "Mask Death Demon", which is a variation on her name that she likes.

Then she will leave you in peace, but don't hang around – she has a terrible memory and will soon be back asking you again. And next time she may not be so forgiving.

"The Meishin Expressway" and "Mask Death Demon". It is worth remembering these phrases. Because it is said that when anyone first becomes aware of the tragic story of Kashima Reiko, they will meet her in one month's time...

FOOLED YOU

This is a true story, so they say. Some say it happened in Arkansas, some in Aberdeen. The people of Montreal swear it happened there. Or maybe near where you are, who knows?

One night a father was sitting down to watch television when he heard his six-year-old son calling out, "Daddy, there's a ghost! Daddy, there's a ghost!"

Ghosts, monsters, there was a different thing every night. "Quiet!" the father called out and went back to watching television.

A minute later, he heard his son again. "Daddy, there's a ghost! Daddy, there's a ghost!"

Now getting angry, the father again shouted, "Quiet!" and went back to his television.

But one more time, "Daddy, there's a ghost! Daddy, there's a ghost!"

This time the father got up and stormed into the room. He saw his son with the sheets pulled up over his head, still calling, "Daddy, there's a ghost! Daddy, there's a ghost!"

Deciding to end the nonsense, the father said to his son, "Where?"

"Under the bed, Daddy! Under the bed!"

The father looked under the bed and there was... his son.

His son looked at him with terror, and said "Daddy, Daddy, there's a ghost ON TOP OF THE BED."

FEATHERSTONE CASTLE

She was not happy to be married, at least not to this man. When she said "I do", she was thinking of another man, a local boy named Ridley, who she truly loved. But that is how it was in seventeenth-century England: if your father, Baron Featherstonehaugh, arranged a marriage for you, you had no choice.

And so Abigail Featherstonehaugh and a local duke were married at Featherstone Castle on 17 January, a bright and pleasant day, by all accounts. A huge banquet was planned for the evening, but first the baron wished his guests to enjoy his magnificent grounds on a hunting expedition while he stayed behind to oversee the preparation of the feast.

The party headed out, bride and groom included. The feast was laid out for their return in a couple of hours, hopefully with more game to add to the pies.

The two hours passed. Then three. Then four. At first the baron was angry, then worried. Darkness fell and he sent a search party out. They returned empty handed. Five hours, then six. All the food went cold.

Then, to his relief, he heard his horses approaching and the hunting party hollering. He went down to greet them and find out what had happened.

What had happened? Reputedly, Abigail's true love, the boy Ridley, could not bear the thought of his Abigail being married. In a densely wooded area called Pinkyn Cleugh, he and his men-at-arms had ambushed the bridal party, to try and steal Abigail away. It was a brutal battle with both sides armed to the teeth and in no mood to back down.

One of the bridal party, they say it was the groom, broke free and, seeing Ridley exposed, drove towards him with his sword. Horrified, Abigail threw herself in front of the sword which ran her through, killing her instantly. In his rage, Ridley killed the duke, and in his misery he killed himself. He had been the last man standing; everyone else had died in the battle.

It was not the hunting party returning but their ghosts. The baron could see their wounds, missing limbs and severed heads. His daughter was there, too, with her belly ripped open by her own husband's sword. The baron, in his arrogance, had failed to listen to the wishes of his beloved daughter, and all had paid the ultimate price for ignoring true love.

It is said that the wedding party visited the baron every 17 January, their screams echoing through the castle, until he died broken-hearted. Many claim to have seen them every 17 January since, either riding back from Pinkyn Cleugh to Featherstone Castle, or in the hall eating the feast they were denied by Ridley's ambush. Only the groom is absent.

But that's not all. Near Pinkyn Cleugh is Raven Stone. Cup-shaped, it is believed to have caught some of Ridley's blood as he died. After the battle, ravens swooped down and ate the carrion of the dead and drank Ridley's blood from the Raven Stone. It is said that every 17 January ravens gather at the stone and drink from it again, before circling the castle calling once again for Ridley's lost love to join him.

Perhaps she has joined him, somewhere in a different world to ours. Perhaps the feast the ghostly wedding party enjoys is for their marriage, and not Abigail's to the duke.

THE PENNSYLVANIA HERMIT

"A pardon, a pardon!"

As William Wilson drove his horse into Hangman's Lot in Chester, Pennsylvania he waved the pardon in his hand. He had travelled 15 miles at top speed and this was his second horse. The first one he had lost as he tried to ride through the icy waters of Schuylkill River after the ferryman had refused his plea to make a special trip.

The horse reared on its hind legs at the sight of William's beloved sister Elizabeth, her body broken. She had been hanged for the crime William held the pardon for. He had arrived moments too late.

The tragic tale of William and Elizabeth Wilson seemed over. But in many ways, it was just beginning.

William had been apprenticed as a stone cutter at the age of 16, in 1768, leaving Elizabeth, his beloved older sister, behind to move 50 miles away to Lancaster. She herself found work in a Philadelphia tavern and was seduced by a guest. She returned home pregnant and soon gave birth to twin boys.

In October that year, 1774, she left home to see the father of her children in nearby Newtown Square. When she returned the boys were gone. A week later their bodies were found buried in the woods. She was arrested for their murders, tried, found guilty and sentenced to hanging.

Elizabeth always maintained that it was the father who had killed the children. William rode back from Lancaster and arranged a stay of execution while he went in search of the true murderer. The new date for Elizabeth's execution was set for 3 January 1776 by the head of the council charged with the investigation, Founding Father Benjamin Franklin. William had no time to lose if he was going to bring in the real culprit. Unable to find him, William fell ill and lost track of time. He thought he had a spare day to return and plead to the council, but he was wrong. He rushed to make his plea on the very day of the execution, 3 January. The council deputy, Charles Biddle, was sympathetic to Elizabeth and handed William a signed piece of paper reading, "Do not execute Wilson until you hear further from council." William leapt on his horse and began his desperate journey. If only the ferryman had allowed him across... but we all know that ferrymen are the auguries of death.

William Wilson was a broken man. Some say that he threw himself on the muddy ground, holding his dead sister and weeping for her, and that when he stood up his hair had turned white and he never spoke another word that was not gibberish.

What is known is that he spent the next few years roaming the west of Pennsylvania. In 1802, his wandering ceased. He spent the last 29 years of his life in Indian Echo Cave and became known as the Pennsylvania Hermit. All he owned was a Bible and some cooking implements. His beard grew long and locals would stare at him. He ignored them.

He died in 1821 and immediately people began to see the ghost of William Wilson riding the 15 miles to Chester and

Hangman's Lot, yelling "Pardon, pardon!" Some say that a sighting of William always portends a violent death in the area, and someone wrongly tried for it.

But others swear they have seen him in his cave, sometimes with Elizabeth and her two baby boys.

UNEXPLAINED DEATHS

Two words that should never appear next to each other are "unexplained" and "deaths". We all want to go quietly, and if not, we'd like at least for there to be some explanation, some way for our loved ones to know what happened in our final moments. Sadly this isn't always the case.

Of course, some unexplained deaths are completely natural – but not many. And some are in no way occult – but there are so many that seem to have this element that there is obviously something going on. Were the people who died already caught up in mysterious practices? Or were they the unlucky victims of some sort of ritual killing? Who chose them and why?

Whether washed up on a beach, found dead around a campfire or decapitated on a park bench, none of the cases have been solved, and none is likely to be. After a time, the trail runs as cold as the body left behind. It is possible that the line between those whose deaths are unexplained and those who come back to haunt is a thin one indeed. Perhaps a message will come from the other side, but probably not.

We will just be left feeling a little bit terrified, and hoping that we will never find ourselves being read about in a book like this…

THE CURSE OF THE PHARAOHS

On 4 November 1922, a young water boy, employed by the British Egyptologist Howard Carter, stumbled on a stone in the Valley of Kings, where Carter's team was searching for ancient Egyptian tombs. The team had begun their investigations before World War One and resumed afterwards but without success. The previous year's efforts had ended in failure, and it was with some difficulty that Carter persuaded his financial backer Lord Carnarvon to pay for another attempt.

The stone the boy had stumbled on was loose. Digging around it, Carter soon discovered something which would change his life. Below the stone was a stairway that led to the greatest discovery in the history of Egyptology – the tomb of Tutankhamun.

Here was the best preserved Egyptian tomb ever discovered. It took three weeks of digging for the excavators to reach the door of the central burial shrine. Carnarvon asked Carter if he could see anything inside, to which Carter is said to have replied, "Yes, wonderful things." Gold. Statues. Gilded furniture. Strange preserved animals. And the mummy of King Tut.

But it was something which none could see which may have been the most important aspect of the tomb. Soon after the tomb was opened, rumours began to circulate about a curse – the Mummy's Curse or the Curse of the Pharaohs. Some said that the curse was written above the central doorway, although Carter always denied it, and it was never found.

Shortly after the tomb was opened, Lord Carnarvon was bitten by a mosquito and mysteriously died. According to Carnarvon's son, at the moment of his death Cairo suffered a massive power outage. Back in England, Carnarvon's dog howled once and dropped dead. When an autopsy was conducted on Tutankhamun, a scar was found on the pharaoh's left cheek, the same spot Lord Carnarvon had been bitten. Soon after, two visitors to the tomb, Carnarvon's half-brother Aubrey Herbert and financier George Jay Gould, both fell ill and died. Sherlock Holmes author and spiritualist Arthur Conan Doyle ascribed the deaths to "elementals" – mythical beings released from the tomb.

But it was what happened next which caused the most consternation. Carter had a pet canary which was a firm favourite of the excavation team. One afternoon Carter sent a messenger to his house to collect the bird. Approaching the house, the messenger heard "an almost human scream". Entering he found that inside the birdcage was a live cobra, a symbol of the pharaohs, in its mouth the dead canary.

Was this a warning to stop the excavations? If so, Carter ignored it. He was unperturbed by encountering a jackal in the desert that resembled Anubis, guardian of the dead in Egyptian mythology. He dismissed the curse as, so he put it, "Tommy rot".

And it is true that while Carter lived for another 16 years after discovering Tutankhamun, others in his party, such as

A. C. Mace and Carter's secretary, Captain The Hon. Richard Bethell, both died within two years, the latter being murdered.

Perhaps Carter had beaten the curse through his sheer doggedness. Or was it something else? When he died, various antiquities taken from the tomb were found hidden in his house, including an amulet thought to protect the owner from evil. Might Howard Carter and Tutankhamun have struck some sort of deal? Perhaps they are laughing together in the afterlife?

THE DEATH OF ELISA LAM

It is not the first creepy thing to happen at the Cecil Hotel in Los Angeles. It has many macabre associations – the "Black Dahlia", Elizabeth Short, was a guest there when she was murdered, and the notorious serial killer Richard "the Night Stalker" Ramirez used it as his base. But perhaps the strangest thing to happen at the Cecil is that on 1 February 2013, a Canadian college student, Elisa Lam, who was staying at the hotel, vanished into thin air.

The LAPD released the last known footage of Elisa. She enters the lift at the Cecil, looking perfectly normal, but then pirouettes, bends at the waist and pushes all the buttons. When the doors fail to close, she again bends at the waist, sticks her head outside and looks left and right, then stands quietly in the lift as before. She puts her back against the wall near the buttons as if hiding, then returns to stand in the doorway.

Next she steps in and out of the lift as if dancing, before again entering and pushing all the buttons and walking back outside, where she makes some bizarre hand gestures. She slowly moves to the left. The lift door closes and Elisa is gone.

At first it was assumed that drugs were involved – her actions certainly seemed to match those of someone on medication. She did have a history of mental illness, but staff at the hotel said she was "outgoing, very lively, very friendly" the whole time she was there. Police searched every part of the hotel they could, including the roof, but found no clues, and the dogs picked up no scent.

On 19 February guests started complaining that there was low water pressure and that the water was black and tasted unusual. The caretaker went up to the roof and checked the tanks. Through the small hatch of one, looking up at him, he saw the body of Elisa Lam.

She was naked, but the clothes she was wearing in the footage were in the tank beside her covered in something like sand. To get her out they had to cut the tank open – the hatch was too small for any human to get through. The tank itself was only half full, a very small amount of water for anyone to drown in.

Most puzzling of all was how she got on the roof and into the tank. There was no lift to the roof, and the only way up was alarmed and watched by CCTV cameras. Even if you did reach the roof without setting off an alarm, you'd have to climb onto the water tank platform, scale a second ladder to the top of the tanks, lift the heavy metal hatch and get inside a hole deliberately too narrow for human access.

A post mortem showed that Elisa's body was bloated from the two weeks in the water tank, but there were no signs of violence or any recreational drug use. There was a small quantity of alcohol in her system, one or two drinks at most.

Chillingly, her online Tumblr continued to update after her death. She may have programmed it to be automatic after she died, although this could not be confirmed. Like so much in the Elisa Lam case, there seemed with each update to be something unworldly going on.

The footage of Elisa Lam continues to circulate, as do theories about what happened.

THE STRANGE CASE OF WILLIAM WALLACE

On 19 January 1931, William Herbert Wallace sat down at the Liverpool Central Chess Club for his weekly game. Wallace was a collections agent for an insurance company and had taught himself to play violin in order to accompany his wife Julia, who was an accomplished pianist. Julia was 17 years her husband's senior and they seemed happy.

That night at the chess club, Wallace was handed a message from a phone call received by the club 25 minutes before he arrived, which asked him to go to 25 Menlove Gardens East the following night to discuss insurance with a man named R. M. Qualtrough. The next night he said goodbye to Julia and took a tramcar to the district, only to find there was no such address. After 45 minutes of asking around, he returned home. Both the front and back doors were locked. Forcing the back door, he finally got it open. Inside he found Julia beaten to death.

Wallace was immediately the prime suspect. Police established he could have posed as "Qualtrough" to send a bogus message via the chess club. It was a convenient excuse. But two things seemed to suggest his innocence. First, such a frenzied attack would have left the perpetrator covered in blood. Wallace looked impeccable as he asked around for 25 Menlove Gardens East. Could he have had time to clean up? That was left in doubt by the evidence of a milk-boy, who had spoken to Julia at 6.30 p.m., only moments before Wallace caught the tramcar.

Despite this, Wallace was found guilty and sentenced to death. According to some people present at the trial, it was Wallace's composure which tipped the scales against him. He seemed indifferent, even after the guilty verdict. But shortly afterwards the verdict was overturned on appeal. Wallace was allowed to walk free.

But who did murder Julia Wallace? Public opinion at the time was firmly of the belief it was Wallace – the errand to 25 Menlove Gardens East stretched all credibility. Wallace wrote in his diary that he received hate mail and physical threats and was worried he might be murdered, perhaps by the same killer. Suffering from an inflamed kidney, he turned down an operation which would have saved his life and died only two years after his wife, next to whom he is buried.

Over the years a number of suspects have been proposed, but the most likely appears to be Richard Gordon Parry, a 22-year-old at the time of the murder, who worked for the same insurance company as Wallace. He was a man of lavish tastes, and it is believed that Wallace was aware that Parry was embezzling money from the firm. When Parry was forced to leave the company "under a cloud" he may have believed Wallace had reported him.

Also, a mechanic who had serviced Parry's car had found a glove soaked in blood in the glovebox. When police interviewed

Parry he did have an alibi for the time, but the girlfriend who said he was with her recanted after Wallace was convicted.

But there are those who say that Wallace's calm and the fact that he seemed to have been in two places at once were clues to something deeper. Even the way he was found guilty and then walked free. And how did he learn to play the violin so well so quickly? Perhaps other forces were at work. We will never know.

DYATLOV PASS INCIDENT

In February 1959, a search party in the Ural Mountains of Soviet Russia made a horrifying discovery. Looking for a ski trekking party of nine, they found a tent that had been badly cut open from the inside. Nine sets of footprints led away from the tent, some of just socks, others a single shoe, most barefoot. The tracks led to a forest, where there was the remains of a small fire. Beside it were two bodies, wearing only underwear. Three more corpses were located nearer the camp, suggesting they had tried to return to the tent. The final four bodies were found months later, hidden deep in the forest. They were wearing more clothes, including some taken from their travelling companions.

This event became known as the Dyatlov Pass incident, named for the group's leader, Igor Dyatlov. Post-mortems of the first six bodies showed they had died of hypothermia, although one of the men had a small fracture of the skull. Three others had fatal injuries, broken skulls and ribs. The wounds weren't external, suggesting their bodies had suffered from a great deal of pressure. A woman was missing her tongue, eyes and lips, while two of the men were without eyeballs and eyebrows. What had happened?!

Some theories were immediately dismissed, such as this was

an attack by local tribesmen or animals. No tracks of either were found, nor any signs of a struggle. This probably means it was not a Yeti, but who knows if they leave tracks? Others were convinced that this was the result of a Soviet science experiment gone wrong and covered up by the authorities, or perhaps an extra-terrestrial intervention. Another group of nearby hikers reported seeing strange orange spheres in the sky on the night of the incident, hovering near where the bodies were found.

What about an avalanche? Most deaths of this sort are down to trekkers being caught by huge volumes of falling snow. But there seemed to be no evidence of this where the bodies were found, as the remains of the fire were still visible, and how would that explain the missing clothes, and the missing eyeballs and tongues? Besides, there have been over 100 trips to the same location as part of the investigation and no avalanche has ever happened there. It's simply not a place where avalanches typically happen.

Might the group have just thought there was an avalanche? Did they hear what sounded like one beginning then panic and run from the tent towards the forest in whatever they were wearing? Having lit the fire, might three of them have tried to go back to the tent but died of hypothermia on the way? This is an area where the Soviets tested parachute mines, so could the group have mistaken the explosions for the start of an avalanche?

To this day, scientists remain baffled. Other theories, such as katabatic winds, which are sudden winds of hurricane-like intensity, or Karman vortexes, which produce panic-inducing sounds, have been offered and rejected. Like avalanches, they might solve part of the puzzle but not all of it.

Many years have passed since the nine trekkers went through their ordeal. Scientists now use computer simulations to see the effects of avalanches on areas like the Urals and bodies such as theirs. And yet the mystery remains as perplexing today as when a group of searchers came upon a tent cut open at the top.

IS OVER

He was found inexplicably dead on a beach in Somerton, South Australia in December 1948. He was not dressed for it – he was wearing a jacket, a red, white and blue tie and brown trousers, socks and shoes. All the labels on his clothes had been cut off. He had no hat, no wallet, no identification. There was an unlit cigarette in his top pocket and a packet of chewing gum in his trouser pocket, next to a second-class rail ticket from Adelaide and a box of matches.

Forensic examiners found him to be in good physical shape, although his spleen was enlarged. No poison was found in his body, nor were there signs of violence. But they were sure this was no natural death, they were sure of that. The coroner was unable to find a cause of death, or identify him. He ordered that the Somerton Man, as he was now known, be embalmed. Future investigations may reveal more.

A few weeks later an unclaimed suitcase was discovered at Adelaide railway station. Certain threads on the clothing in the case positively matched those on the dead man. Some of the garments were labelled "T. Keane". The suitcase also contained an electrician's screwdriver and a stencilling brush. But there was no "T. Keane" reported missing across the English-speaking world. Who was this man?

It was then that the case took on an even more mysterious turn. During the inquest, a rolled-up piece of paper was found sewn into the dead man's trouser pocket. The paper had printed on it "*Tamám Shud*", which means "Is Over" and appears on the last page of the famous Persian book, *Rubaiyat of Omar Khayyam*. Police launched a public appeal to try and find the copy of the book from which the page was torn.

Once they located it, the mystery only deepened. Inside the book were five lines written by hand – one crossed out – and they appeared to be in code: a series of random capital letters. Experts and amateurs would spend years trying to crack the code, thwarted by the brevity of the message – if it was a message. But the rumours about the man only multiplied over the years. This was just after World War Two and the start of the Cold War – codes meant spies, and spies meant foreign powers. Could this be the secret of the dead man?

And there was one last clue – a phone number written in the same hand. It turned out to belong to Jessica Thomson, a nurse who lived nearby. Under questioning Jessica claimed not to know the man, or to know why he had written down her number. But some who were present when she was shown a plaster cast of his face said she reacted with shock. Still, she denied knowing the Somerton Man.

Over the years many men have been posited as the Somerton Man, the most recent – and likely – theory being that he was Carl "Charles" Webb, an electrical engineer. But this has not satisfied some paranormal investigators, who note that the facial expression of the man, whoever he was, mirrors what they dub the "Innsmouth Look": bulging eyes, shrivelled neck, flat nose and wide mouth with thick lips. The people of Innsmouth, written about by the horror writer H. P. Lovecraft, are allegedly the descendants of humans and Deep Ones – an ancient race who once ruled over humanity and who undergo a very slow transformation that might take most of a human lifespan to complete.

Is "Tamám Shud" really just a chance phrase, or could it have a deeper meaning? Maybe, in fact, this case is not closed, not by a long way.

WHAT WE DO KNOW AND WHAT WE DON'T

We still do not know, because accounts vary. But do accounts vary to stop us knowing?

Some say when 16-year-old Jeannette DePalma's body was found in a quarry in Springfield, New Jersey, her skeletal remains were surrounded by occult objects. But others say there were no such items or that she was inside a coffin-shaped perimeter with crosses all around it. Others claim that she was in a pentagram – a five-pointed star once used to signify the wound of Jesus, now used in contemporary pagan ceremonies. Certain theories contend that around the pentagram were animal remains, others that there were not. Still others do not even attest to the presence of a pentagram.

We do know that she left her parents' home six weeks earlier to take a train to a friend's house. We do know that it was the last time she was seen alive. We do know there were no drugs involved and that the coroner believed she had been strangled. We also know that missing from her body were her purse and a cross necklace of no great value.

We do know that the Springfield Police Department claimed for 25 years they had lost the case files in a hurricane and that it turned out to be untrue.

What we don't know is who did this to Jeannette DePalma, and why.

CAUSE UNKNOWN

The assignment was called "Navigation Problem No. 1" and it was supposed to be a routine practice bombing operation. Lieutenant Charles Carroll Taylor had over 2,500 flying hours clocked and his trainees on Flight 19 were experienced pilots. The five aeroplanes and 14 crew members leaving Florida would be back in a few hours.

That was 5 December 1945. We are still waiting for them.

We know the practice run was safely completed, the last bomb being dropped at 3 p.m. But at 3.45, when the planes should have been approaching the airfield, the first signs of trouble began. Fort Lauderdale's flight tower received a message from Taylor, who sounded confused and worried. "Cannot see land," he said. "We seem to be off course." The flight tower asked where they were. "We cannot be sure where we are," the flight leader announced. "Repeat: Cannot see land."

There was silence for 10 minutes, then another message, but not from Taylor. "We can't find west. Everything is wrong. We can't be sure of any direction. Everything looks strange, even the ocean." After another 20 minutes, a hysterical voice said, "We can't tell where we are... everything is... can't make out anything. We think we may be about 225 miles northeast of base..." There was some mumbling and then the final words that flight control ever received from Flight 19: "It looks like we are entering white water… We're completely lost."

Two PBM Mariner flying boats carrying 13 men and rescue equipment were scrambled for Flight 19's last estimated position. Ten minutes later, they sent a message relaying their position. They were never heard from again. In a few hours, seven search planes and 27 men had disappeared into thin air. For five days the searches continued in the 250,000 square miles formed by the triangle of Florida, Puerto Rico and Bermuda. None of the aircraft were found, and the US Air Force report said simply "cause unknown".

So was born the legend of the Bermuda Triangle. Numerous ships had previously vanished in the area, but there was always a rational explanation. To lose so many aircraft and so many men in one go was unprecedented.

More losses followed. In 1948 and 1949, the Star Tiger and Star Ariel disappeared between Jamaica and Bermuda with a loss of over 50 souls. Then a Douglas DC-3 went down with 32 passengers. In 1963, two KC-135 Stratotankers "collided" – yet according to some, two sets of debris were found 160 miles apart. And another half-dozen small planes have come down there since. No other region on Earth has seen so many mysterious fatalities.

A number of natural explanations have been proposed, from magnetic variations which affect compasses, to hurricane activity, violent weather and even undersea bubbles dragging planes and ships down. But none of these seem to account for the frequency of the deaths, or the way they happened.

Did the pilots of Flight 19 experience something science cannot describe? Some have proposed that the Bermuda Triangle is a parallel universe, causing a warp in time and space which sucks victims in. Or could it be that the Bermuda Triangle is a hotspot of extra-terrestrial activity?

There is one other possibility. In 1968, three divers off the coast of Bimini Island discovered rock formations which looked suspiciously like manmade walls and pavements. Could it be that here, lurking in the depths of the seas near where Flight 19 disappeared, is the Lost City of Atlantis? Could it be causing disturbances?

Or could it be repopulating?

THE PRINCES IN THE TOWER

On 9 April 1483, Edward IV, King of England, died suddenly. He had two sons, 12-year-old Edward and nine-year-old Richard. On the death of his father, Edward was due to become the new monarch, Edward V. All that was left was to crown him, and he and his brother travelled to London for the coronation. Edward IV had appointed his younger brother – their uncle – Richard, Duke of Gloucester, as the Lord Protector, to mentor and advise the young king. Richard did not remain Duke of Gloucester for long – we now know him as the villainous Richard III.

Arriving in London, the princes were placed in the Tower of London as was traditional for princes awaiting coronation. But while they were there, Richard had them declared illegitimate and crowned himself king. The princes were never seen again.

Had they been murdered on the orders of Richard? Many have thought so, including Shakespeare, but no evidence has been found for the dastardly deed, and no one in the Tower ever confessed or produced any evidence. Could they have escaped or have been rescued? Again, there is no evidence, but the story then took a strange turn.

Richard III himself was killed in battle with Henry VII at the Battle of Bosworth in 1485. Ten years later, a young man arrived in England claiming to be the younger prince. He said his older brother had been murdered, but the executioners had taken pity on him and exiled him to mainland Europe. He had promised not to reveal his true identity. "Perkin Warbeck", as he was now known, had lived under the protection of Edward IV's loyalists, and was now returning to reclaim the throne.

Supported by several European kings and emperors, he arrived in Kent in 1495. Henry VII engaged him in battle, forcing him to flee to Scotland, where the king of that nation, James IV, provided him with arms and men for a second coup attempt. His promises to lower taxes were well received and he gained wide popular support. However, Henry VII again defeated him. Imprisoned in the very Tower of London he claimed to have been freed from years earlier, he soon confessed that he was an imposter. But soon after that he escaped, claiming once again to be the true king. This time when he was arrested, he was put to death. Four centuries later, Mary Shelley, the author of *Frankenstein*, would write a novel about him, *The Fortunes of Perkin Warbeck*, sealing his macabre place in English history.

And what of the princes?

On 17 July 1674, workmen at the Tower of London dug up a wooden box containing two small human skeletons, wrapped in velvet, possibly signifying royalty. The bones were reinterred at Westminster Abbey and a monument erected. In 1933 they were dug up and analysed, the results inconclusive. Apart from being mixed in with chicken and other animal parts, many bones were missing, and the tests were not thorough. Some have suggested that there was little appetite for establishing their true identity. Another cover-up?

Calls for another examination of the remains have grown since 2014, when a skeleton found beneath a car park was confirmed as belonging to Richard III. Some believe it would be fitting to confirm that the princes ended up in Westminster Abbey and their likely murderer underneath a municipal car park.

Unless the true prince lies beneath a stone marked "Perkin Warbeck"?

FORTY-TWO DAYS

On 8 February 1981, a young homeless man, Leroy Carter Jr., was found dead on the bench he had been sleeping on in the Golden Gate Park, San Francisco. He was still in his sleeping bag, surrounded by a pool of blood.

What made the attack particularly grisly was that not only had Carter's head been cut off, but it was missing. It had been done with precision. As the coroner later wrote, "The cut was very clean, like an expert did it." Even more disturbing, a chicken wing had been forced into Carter's neck-hole along with some kernels of corn. Fifty yards away police found a headless chicken, with the same wing missing.

The police report was to the point. "It appears the victim was sleeping in the bushes... when person or persons unknown to us at this time came along and decapitated him." The police enlisted the help of Officer Sandi Gallant, who had recently been working on the case of Jim Jones, the messianic cult leader who had ordered his followers to kill themselves in what became known as the Jonestown Massacre. In order to carry out her investigations into Jones, Gallant had become something of an expert in cults and satanic rituals.

She researched black magic beliefs that may have provided clues, and came across the Palo Mayombe cult, which mixed

Aztec blood rites, Haitian voodoo, Catholicism and sometimes devil worship. It was a form of Santería, a creed that originated in Nigeria 500 years ago. It arrived in the Americas via slave ships.

Human sacrifice was not generally part of its ritual practices, although animal sacrifice was. There had been incidents, though, that bore an uncanny resemblance to the decapitation of Leroy Carter.

As Gallant told the police department, it was not understanding the decapitation that was so important to solving the case, it was why the head had been obtained. The head – eyes, ears and brain included – would be used to make a ritualistic brew which would then be consumed. This process would take 21 days. And then 21 days after that the leftover skull would be returned. As she later told the *LA Times*, "At the end of those 21 days, if the priest deemed it appropriate, he would actually sleep in an area with this head and with this cauldron for another 21-day period. Then on the 42nd day he discards the head… in close proximity to where he took it from. To him, that was a sacred way of returning the head."

But that was old magic, and this was the twentieth-century United States. So even Sandi Gallant was sceptical, and the police preferred to use traditional methods to seek the killer.

Which is why, on 22 March 1981, 42 days after the victim had been killed, there was no police officer anywhere near where he had been found. If there was, they might have seen the person who placed the decomposed head of Leroy Carter Jr. back next to where they had taken it from.

KA-BOOM!

On 2 July 1951, the landlady of 67-year-old Mary Reeser's apartment in Florida noticed that the doorknob was hot. When she couldn't wake her lodger she contacted police, who arrived shortly after and forced open the door. What they saw inside appalled them.

On an overstuffed easy chair in the apartment were Mary's charred remains – part of her left foot was still wearing a slipper and her backbone was "baked into" the upholstery. Among the ashes around the chair her skull was found, shrunken, apparently, to the "size of a teacup". Nothing else in the apartment was burned, although several plastic items near the body had melted.

The police were bewildered. While the paint higher up on the walls had cracked, the walls lower down were pristine. Her untouched newspaper beside the charred remains was in perfect condition, as were the sheets in her bedroom – clean and white. All the normal signs of a fire were missing, apart from Mary's badly burned body.

The case gripped the American imagination. Was this a freak lightning strike or some hi-tech new ray gun used to kill this seemingly innocent widow? Some blamed napalm, or a fire ball which came through the window. "I seen it happen before," wrote one man to the local newspaper.

The chief of police J. R. Reichart wrote to the head of the FBI, J. Edgar Hoover. "Dear Mr. Hoover. This fire is too puzzling for the small-town force to handle." He sent with his letter portions of the apartment rug, rubble from the walls and floor, smoke samples and segments of the chair.

The investigation was inconclusive – it could only say what hadn't happened. It wasn't lightning or napalm or a fireball, and ray guns don't exist – they said. That left one possibility that a number of correspondents had raised with the press. Spontaneous human combustion, known to paranormal investigators as SHC.

Stories of SHC go back years. The author of *Moby-Dick*, Herman Melville, claimed to have witnessed one at sea. Charles Dickens wrote about it in *Bleak House*. In the nineteenth century hundreds of cases were reported and, as many of those who died were female and overweight it was put down to a "debauched" lifestyle. And as recently as 2010, the death of a man in Ireland was ruled as SHC by the coroner.

In the case of Mary Reeser, the authorities suspected the fact that she was a heavy smoker contributed to what happened. Scientists pointed to the wick effect, where a person is slowly burned when their body fat is ignited. The body becomes like a candle, but inside out – the body fat is like the wax, the wick is effectively their clothing. If the victim is intoxicated they may be slow to react to the growing heat. Could Mary Reeser have dropped a cigarette on herself and slowly burned to death? In the end the FBI decided that this was the case.

But Wilton M. Krogman, an anthropologist from the University of Pennsylvania, disagreed, as many have since. "I cannot conceive of such complete cremation without more burning in the apartment," Krogman said. The debate about SHC and the death of Mary Reeser continues to this day.

Reeser's family were satisfied with the FBI investigation and later told the local paper they could still feel her presence in the apartment. When visitors felt a strange breeze, her family would simply say, "That's Grandma. Don't worry, she's nice."

THE HOUSE OF LAMENTS

It is not how they died that is unexplained, but who they were, and how many.

Some say that when his wife Constanza was killed in a violent assault in Guanajuato, Mexico in the 1890s, it pushed mine-owner Tadeo Mejía over the edge, sending him mad. Others say it is worse, that he remained perfectly sane.

Whichever is the case, they say at the Casa de los Lamentos – the House of Laments – you can reputedly still hear the groans and shrieks of Mejía's victims.

Apparently, after Constanza's death, Mejía consulted a local witch to ask how he could bring her back. The witch advised human sacrifices, and Mejía agreed. He would lure people of all ages back to the House of Laments, and they would never be seen again. His final victim was himself, possibly in despair that the advice of the witch proved ill-founded, or possibly because it worked and Constanza summoned him over.

After he died, in the basement they found hundreds of human remains, along with Satanic imagery and implements of black magic.

It is now a tourist destination, of course, where, if you listen carefully, it is said you can hear the laments of the dead. In the kitchen you can see family photographs, as well as the very plates that Constanza and Mejía ate from together, and cups they must have shared and which, legend has it, were used to collect blood once she was gone...

THE LOST COLONY
OF ROANOKE

Sir Walter Raleigh is probably best known for introducing tobacco to England, but he was also responsible for one of the most enigmatic disappearances in world history, the 115 colonists of the first English settlement in North America. Even after almost 500 years, the Lost Colony of Roanoke remains a baffling mystery.

In 1578, Queen Elizabeth I granted a royal charter to colonize territories "unclaimed by Christian kingdoms". Raleigh was tasked with establishing a North American colony. Forbidden from leaving the queen's side, he organized the missions remotely.

In 1585, a fleet of seven ships under the command of Sir Richard Grenville left Plymouth for the New World, heading south through the Bay of Biscay. Rotten luck meant that the ships encountered storms everywhere, many of the settlers left the mission to become privateers and the main supply ship, the *Tiger*, ran into a shoal and sank, ruining most of the provisions. Without supplies, the settlers would be heavily dependent on the generosity of the natives.

Eventually they made it to Roanoke, off the coast of what is now North Carolina, determined to establish a new colony to bring Christianity to this heathen land.

They also planned to study the natives. As the colony was being established, Grenville and his men visited a local group of Secotan people. When they returned, it seems a silver cup they had taken to show the natives had vanished. Grenville and his men believed it was stolen, and returned to burn down the town and its crops. Later researchers would wonder whether a curse was put on them in return.

Gradually the colony began to trade with the indigenous populations, buying corn and other supplies. But the colonists noticed a disturbing problem. Each village they visited seemed to suffer a deadly epidemic afterwards. Tensions rose. The colonists needed both supplies and reinforcements.

It was eventually decided that the governor of the new colony, John White, would return to England and raise a new fleet. He left behind his daughter, Virginia, and granddaughter, Eleanor, the first settler child born on Roanoke.

Two years later, on 18 August 1590, his granddaughter's third birthday, White returned with six ships given to him by Raleigh, full of fresh provisions. He was surprised when no colonists greeted his arrival. When he had left the colony it had been bustling, but now a distressing silence met him as he made land. In the sand he found fresh footprints and continued into the island. But the colony was gone. Every building. Every supply. And every single person.

The only thing left was the word "CROATOAN" carved in one of the posts. It was the name of a nearby island. White thought the colonists may have relocated, but subsequent searches showed otherwise. The colony of Roanoke was gone.

There have been many investigations and many theories. Were they killed by the natives? Archaeologists have searched for bones but found none, which also rules out an epidemic. Might they have attempted to return to England and been lost at sea? They had been left one ship, but experts agree it was not big enough for all of them, let alone supplies, so what happened to the rest? Others have proposed freak weather, a Spanish attack or assimilation with the Native Americans. No theory seems to explain it.

John White retired to one of Raleigh's estates, spending his remaining years painting watercolours and awaiting the return of his precious girls, Virginia and Eleanor.

THE UNKNOWN WOMAN OF THE SEINE

Paris. The city of love. Where handsome men fall in love with beautiful women, and their love is obsessive. There is no greater city for tragic love affairs or, as it is called locally, *l'amour fou*.

But what if a whole city falls in love with one woman? And what if that love spreads around the whole world? No female has been as widely and compulsively loved as *L'Inconnue de la Seine* – the Unknown Woman of the Seine.

In the late 1880s, the body of a young female was pulled from the River Seine. Nobody knew who she was or how she had died. There were no external injuries, and so most agreed it was suicide – it was not uncommon in those days for a jilted lover to choose death over sorrow. *"C'est comme ça"* as they say in French with a shrug. "That's how it is."

But what happened next was extraordinary. A pathologist at the Paris Morgue was so taken by the woman's beauty he made a plaster death mask of her. It showed she was aged between 16 and 20, with pronounced cheekbones, a high forehead and, most striking of all, a serenely happy expression, her mouth curled up in an enigmatic smile like, as many noted, the famous painting the *Mona Lisa* hanging nearby in the Louvre.

Some said her expression was so peaceful she cannot have been a suicide, others thought the mask a fake, taken from the daughter of a German mask manufacturer.

Thousands of copies of the mask were made and they grew popular in Parisian bars and cafés. Literary works and paintings immortalized L'Inconnue de la Seine, a ballet was written in her honour and France's most celebrated photographer, Man Ray, made studies of her in the 1960s.

But it was not just France that was in love with her. Her first literary mention was in an 1899 British novel, *The Worshipper of the Image*, in which a poet falls in love with the woman, prompting his wife to commit suicide. L'Inconnue de la Seine has been the subject of Czech, Russian and German novels. A 1936 German film, *Die Unbekannte* (*The Unknown*), tells her story before she drowned – she was Madeleine, a night club singer who committed suicide after finding out that her lover had a fiancée.

But that was not the strangest part of her fame. In 1958, the Austrian physician Peter Safar and the American physician James Elam wished to develop a tool to teach emergency workers and members of the general public how to perform mouth-to-mouth resuscitation. They asked the famous Norwegian doll maker Asmund Laerdal to design a mannikin for them that people would feel comfortable placing their mouths on. He had seen a plaster cast of L'Inconnue de la Seine at the house of his in-laws and thought it perfect.

And so L'Inconnue de la Seine had a second life, as the famous "Resusci Annie", who has taught many generations of people throughout the world mouth-to-mouth resuscitation. We don't know how she died, but according to many this mysterious woman of the Seine now has "the most kissed lips in history".

However she died, this mysterious girl has, according to Laerdal's company, saved over two million lives. Perhaps we have an explanation for that smile.

MONEY TROUBLES

As Elvis Presley proved, going to the lavatory can be a fatal business. History is littered with people whose demise occurred while engaged in such business. Duke Jing of Jin fell into a toilet pit in 581 BCE. George II of England went to his water closet and never returned in 1760. Others have been assassinated in the latrine, including Godfrey the Hunchback (by spear in 1076) and the celebrated Japanese warrior Uesugi Kenshin (by ninja, 1578). On some occasions several people have lost their lives, such as in the toilet malfunction on the German submarine *U-1206* (flooded, 1945) or the Erfurt latrine disaster of 1184 (don't ask).

But the toilet-related mortality which had the greatest impact on world affairs remains a puzzle. When the Belgian financier Alfred Loewenstein boarded his private plane on 4 July 1928, with five other people including the pilot, he was the third richest man in the world, with investments in electric power and the silk industry.

Halfway through the flight across the English Channel, on his way from England to Brussels, Loewenstein went to the rear of the aircraft to relieve himself. The plane had two doors at the rear: one to the toilet and another an exit. When Loewenstein had been missing for 10 minutes, his valet, Fred Baxter, went

123

in search of him. According to Baxter, the toilet was empty and the exit door open. There was no sign of Loewenstein.

The case was immediately suspicious. The exit door was virtually impossible for one man to open, let alone jump out through given both the cabin pressure and the force of the wind outside. The pilots chose not to land at the nearest available airfield, but carried on to a beach at Dunkirk where there happened to be an army unit training. The main pilot, Donald Drew, was evasive when questioned about his boss's disappearance both at the time and later on.

News of the death sent shockwaves through the stock market, Loewenstein's corporations' shares falling by 50 per cent. Arguably these were the first tremors of the Great Depression which would strike the following year.

Loewenstein's body washed up near Boulogne two weeks later, and was identified because of his wristwatch. A post-mortem revealed a cracked skull and other broken bones but concluded he had been alive when he hit the water. No poison was detected, nor any injuries inconsistent with a fall from that height into water.

To this day we don't know what happened. Some speculate he committed suicide in the knowledge that some of his more tangled business investments were about to come undone. He owed a lot of investors a lot of money.

Or was it murder? One or more of the investors may have grown tired of waiting, while another theory argues that Loewenstein had recently become involved in the opiate trade.

Others have proposed that it was a sort of occult sacrifice. The plane's other passengers behaved suspiciously before and after the incident and at least one was known to have ties to a secret society. Perhaps Loewenstein himself had dabbled – the opiate business at that time had some strange players.

Or perhaps the simplest explanation is the best. Alfred Loewenstein, the third richest man in the world, lost everything while trying to spend a penny.

THE CURSE OF SUPERMAN

"He's probably going to go shoot himself," she said. There was a noise upstairs. She continued, "He's opening a drawer to get the gun." A shot rang out. "See there – I told you so!"

When American socialite Leonore Lemmon was interviewed by police about her fiancé's death in June 1959, three days before their marriage, she was as cool as you'd expect a Hollywood socialite to be. She also lived up to her reputation for toughness – she was the only woman ever barred from the exclusive Stork Club for starting a fist fight. Nor was her fiancé an ordinary man. He was George Reeves, Superman.

Which is a dangerous thing to be. The "Curse of Superman" has apparently stricken so many actors over the years that many have been reluctant to take the role, or any other role in a Superman production. George's near-namesake Christopher Reeve was paralyzed after falling from a horse. His co-star Margot Kidder, who played love interest Lois Lane, took her own life. Even the boy who played the baby in the 1978 film died of a heart attack aged 14.

But George Reeves was the first to be cursed. His death was reported as suicide. His career had tanked in the six years since he stopped playing Superman and he was in financial difficulties. Denied other roles, he was reduced to cameos as Man of Steel on shows like *I Love Lucy*, despite only being in his late forties. "Here I am," he'd say, "wasting my life."

After years of obscurity, he had been offered the role of Superman in 1951. Reluctant at first, he eventually signed and was catapulted into national celebrity. The audience loved the show, and Reeves paid special attention to young fans, making himself a role model and keeping his personal life private, including his affair with Toni Mannix, wife of MGM general manager Eddie Mannix. But after two years Reeves was dissatisfied with the part, and the producers' failure to raise his salary. He quit.

It turned out to be a mistake. When he retired to his bedroom during a party at his house on 16 June 1959, sometime between 1.30 and 2 a.m., Leonore Lemmon, as she told the police, knew what he was going to do. George Reeves was going to shoot himself.

Or was he? As soon as he died, questions were being asked about how and why. According to guests, Reeves had barely attended the party, going to bed early and only coming down once to complain about the noise. Or was it twice? No one could really remember. As the police put it, everyone else there was extremely inebriated.

He had been discovered naked on the bed in a pool of blood, gore sprayed up the wall. But why were his fingerprints not on the gun, nor any residue on his hands? And why were there three bullet holes, the one that killed Reeves in the ceiling, the others in the floor?

Years later, Phyllis Coates, who had played Lois Lane on the show, said she received a call at 4.30 a.m. on the night Reeves died from his ex, Toni. She said, "The boy is dead.

He's been murdered." Did her husband Eddie, with Mafia ties, have Reeves murdered? Or do it himself?

Perhaps this was not a case of the Curse of Superman, but the story of a jealous husband, whose revenge was a dish best served cold.

THE BENNINGTON TRIANGLE

If you ever find yourself in southwestern Vermont, one area you might want to avoid is Bennington, especially between about three and four in the afternoon, and *especially* if you are wearing red.

This patch of woodland is purportedly one of the oddest places on Earth – between 1945 and 1950 there were at least six unsolved disappearances, all around Glastenbury Mountain, earning this 58 square mile area the nickname "the Bennington Triangle". Only two bodies were ever found – those of Carl Herrick and Frieda Langer.

Herrick was out shooting with his brother Henry in November 1943 when the pair got separated. Henry called in vain, then went to get help. It took several days to locate the body. Carl's gun was beside it with no bullets discharged. A post-mortem determined that he died from his ribs puncturing his lung. Death by squeezing.

After a second death the townsfolk grew concerned. Seventy-four-year-old Middie Rivers was hiking with friends in November 1945 on a trail very familiar to him. Rivers was fit, so no one worried when he went ahead of them. Despite a month of searching, which turned up one of his rifle cartridges, Middie was never found.

A year later, 18-year-old Paula Jean Welden, a college sophomore, set out on a Bennington's Long Trail, wearing a distinctive red coat. She was seen a few hours later by an elderly couple also hiking on the trail – and then never seen again. A four-week search found no trace of her.

With three instances in three years, rumours began to circulate about the woodland. Was there a serial killer? Or some sort of paranormal activity? What had squeezed Carl Herrick to death? And why were all the deaths around the same time?

But Bennington remained popular, and three years passed without incident. Then something even more mysterious occurred. James Telford, a 68-year-old army veteran, boarded a bus to Bennington to visit relatives. Fourteen passengers confirmed that he did not get off the bus before Bennington – and yet when the bus arrived at its destination, Telford was gone. His belongings were still on his seat.

Eight-year-old Pula Jepson was, like Paula Jean Welden, wearing a red coat when his mother left him in her truck near Bennington while she fed some pigs. When she returned, he was gone. A pack of bloodhounds tracked down the dead boy in the woodlands – in the exact same spot where Welden was last seen.

Sixteen days later, 53-year-old Frieda Langer and her cousin Herbert Elsner were hiking in the woods when Frieda slipped in a stream. She told Herbert she would go back to their tent and change out of her wet clothes, then catch up with him. Herbert waited by the stream for a while then went back to the campsite. Frieda was gone. Some 300 locals and police trawled the area around the campsite, but she wasn't found – until seven months later, only three and a half miles from the campsite, an area which had been extensively searched. The cause of death could not be ascertained – her remains were too badly damaged.

Not long after, Glastenbury and nearby Somerset became ghost towns – the local economy gradually collapsed. The deaths ended. Then in 2019 a murdered woman was found near Somerset reservoir. In 2021 a young man was discovered dead in his truck. The truck was red, as was the nickname of the dead woman, Jessica "Red" Hildebrandt.

Coincidence?

THE STRANGE CASE OF PAULINE PICARD

On a quiet day in April 1922, in Brittany, France, two-year-old Pauline Picard went to play outside with her siblings, as she did most days in this remote farmland. There was nothing, it seemed, to worry about.

Several hours later, her mother called the children in. They all came – apart from Pauline. There was a search of the area by 150 people, but to no avail.

Days passed and rumours mounted about who had taken her. An animal? A murderer?

Then her parents received a call. A two-year-old matching Pauline's description had been found in Cherbourg – 300 miles away. They travelled there and were overjoyed: it was Pauline. She was oddly silent and distant, but her parents ascribed this to trauma. The news went global.

But then things became strange. When Pauline did start talking, she didn't use the Breton dialect she grew up speaking. A local farmer, Yves Martin, saw the girl, screamed "God help me, I am guilty" and ran away, never to be seen again. It slowly dawned on the Picards that this was not their daughter.

Two weeks later, their doubts were confirmed. The mutilated body of a girl was found. Nearby clothes matched Pauline's. Next to the clothes was a skull.

But it was the skull of an adult man.

So who was the girl now at the Picards'? All efforts to find out failed and the traumatized Picards sent her to an orphanage. Records reveal that this girl died months later from measles.

Who murdered Pauline? And who did the skull belong to? The remains had not been there when the first search happened, that was clear. Had they been murdered together? Separately? Was the man murdered at all? No adult male was missing locally.

A hundred years on, the conundrums of Pauline Picard, Yves Martin, the girl from Cherbourg and the man's skull have never been solved, not even the question of whether any of them were even linked. It seems unlikely they ever will be.

THAT'LL BE THE DAY (THAT I DIE)

He was the biggest rock and roll star of the time, and perhaps the first rock star. When Buddy Holly's aeroplane crashed during a tour of the midwestern states on 3 February 1959 even those who thought that rock and roll was the Devil's music were stunned. That also among the dead were the 17-year-old singer of "La Bamba", Ritchie Valens, and another new idol, the Big Bopper, sent shockwaves through the music world.

The explanation for the crash seemed simple. Buddy Holly and his band the Crickets had finished a show at the Surf Ballroom in Iowa just before midnight and were supposed to drive to their next gig. The Crickets' drummer, Carl Bunch, had been hospitalized and was not able to travel with his bandmates. He would later feel like the luckiest man in the world, given the tragedy that would befall the Crickets. The weather was dangerously icy, so Holly rented a Beechcraft Bonanza plane. But it was too small to fit everyone. Crickets guitarist Waylon Jennings gave up his seat to the Big Bopper, who was suffering from the flu. Then the other Crickets guitarist Tommy Allsup tossed a coin with Ritchie Valens to see who would take the last seat. Valens "won". Valens was unhappy – he had a fear of planes, having seen two collide above his school when he was a boy. But he reluctantly joined Holly and the Big Bopper on the plane.

Shortly after take-off the plane crashed into a frozen cornfield. The three rock stars and the pilot all died on impact. It seemed a simple case of a too-small plane going down in conditions that should have prevented it from ever going up.

Enter Joe Meek.

Meek was a 1950s record producer who, as late as 2012, the music magazine *NME* was calling the greatest record producer of all time. His biggest hit, "Telstar", performed by the Tornados, was the first UK song to go to Number One in the US. His music was described as "space age" and "out of this world".

He also dabbled in the occult. At one Tarot reading in 1958 he heard that Buddy Holly would die on 3 February that year. He contacted Holly, who was touring the UK – Holly laughed it off. And sure enough, 3 February came and went. Meek had been wrong – about the year, at least.

After Holly's death, Meek became obsessed with the singer. Thinking he was able to communicate with the dead, he told people that Holly talked to him in his dreams, blaming him for getting the year wrong, but also helping him write songs. He produced a song called "Tribute to Buddy Holly". It was a flop as listeners found it too morbid.

Meek started to believe that his flat in London was filled with poltergeists and that he could control the minds of his musicians. He also stopped using his telephone as he believed his landlady, Violet Shenton, was eavesdropping on him down the chimney.

In 1967, police were called to his flat in Holloway Road, London. Meek had shot his landlady and turned the gun on himself. The date was 3 February.

Mourners still visit the cornfield where Buddy Holly, Ritchie Valens and the Big Bopper fell to Earth. Some report hearing screaming. Others have supposedly taken photographs that show strange balls of light. Perhaps it was as straightforward as a small plane defeated by bad weather. Or was Joe Meek onto something?

THE PITCHFORK MURDER

They called him Fabian of the Yard and even made a television series about his investigations. Chief Inspector Robert Fabian of England's Scotland Yard was the best sleuth in the business. But even he couldn't crack a murder that had happened in Warwickshire on Valentine's Day 1945.

When 74-year-old agricultural worker Charles Walton's fully dressed corpse was found near a hedgerow, his own bill-hook, used for cutting hedges, had been forced into his upper neck. Below it, his pitchfork had been driven through his throat with such force that the prongs had been bent back by the frozen ground.

A little way off, they found his walking stick covered in blood and hair, indicating he had been beaten viciously with it. He had obviously been cutting the hedge – it was nearly done, the rest would have taken about half an hour before he was due to head home.

The main suspect was Walton's employer, Albert Potter, who had a fiery temper and mistreated his staff. When Fabian interrogated him, his story kept changing. But more evidence was needed. Fabian then interviewed everyone who was close to Walton.

This was when things became eerie. No one would talk to

him. Even so, Fabian was able to establish Walton's movements before the murder, which were unremarkable. What *was* remarkable was that, although Walton was fully dressed, closer examination revealed that his fly was undone and his trousers open. Whether, as rumour had it, there was a cross carved into the dead body's chest, Fabian would never confirm or deny.

Had Walton been killed in some sort of occult ritual? Fabian heard rumours that Walton was known locally as some sort of witch, who put the evil eye on other farms, causing them to have poor harvests. In 1944, all the neighbouring farms had suffered, but not Alfred Potter's. Valentine's Day is also the day of the pagan festival of Imbolc, signifying the start of spring. Was Walton's blood spilt as a sacrifice?

And then there was the vexed issue of how he was killed and where. It was soon revealed that in 1875 there had been another murder in this village at almost the same spot. The victim was Ann Tennant. The killer claimed she was a witch and murdered her in broad daylight – with a pitchfork. Walton was possibly Tennant's great-grandson. Had her murderer been correct and Walton had inherited her black magic powers?

Finally, there were the black dogs. It was rumoured that one was found hanging by the murder site shortly after Walton's death. Fabian himself saw several running around when he visited, but when he asked a local boy about them he turned pale and ran away.

Walton's murder was never solved. Perhaps it had nothing to do with the occult – close-knit communities are driven by gossip. But the last words should go to Fabian, who was not only known for his investigative skill but for being the most level-headed of men.

He wrote, "I advise anybody who is tempted at any time

to venture into Black Magic, witchcraft, Shamanism – call it what you will – to remember Charles Walton and to think of his death, which was clearly the ghastly climax of a pagan rite. There is no stronger argument for keeping as far away as possible from the villains with their swords, incense and mumbo-jumbo. It is prudence on which your future peace of mind and even your life could depend."

WHO PUT BELLA IN THE WYCH-ELM?

On 18 April 1943, four boys were playing in Hagley Wood, Worcestershire, England, and saw a wych-elm tree. They decided to look for birds' nests in it. Fifteen-year-old Bob Farmer climbed up to look inside the hollow trunk. There was no nest. Instead there was a female skeleton, complete except for a missing hand.

The terrified boys swore each other to secrecy and ran home, but the youngest was in such a state that he told his father. Police rushed to the wych-elm. The woman still had some hair hanging from the flesh of her head but only two teeth left. The severed hand was found buried nearby, as were her clothes.

The woman was identified as being 35–40 years old and had been in the tree for about 18 months. It was ascertained she had been placed in the tree while still warm.

Rumours spread that she had been part of a witches' coven and had died during a satanic ritual, which may have included the Hand of Glory – in which a killer's hand is removed before they are executed giving it supernatural powers.

Furthermore, wych-elms have long been associated with death and melancholy, and their wood used for coffins. Could this be part of the puzzle?

Nobody knows who the missing woman was, although a short time later, graffiti started appearing in the area reading: "Who put Bella in the wych-elm?"

Is it possible that someone did know her true identity?

THE YOG'TZE MYSTERY

At almost 11 p.m. on 25 October 1984 in Anzhausen, Germany, Günther Stoll leapt from his chair and shouted to his wife, "*Jetzt geht mir ein Licht auf!*" – "Now I've got it!"

He grabbed a piece of paper and wrote down six letters, YOG'TZE, before immediately crossing them out. He then fled the house. A few hours later he'd be dead, in a mystery which continues to mystify German authorities.

For some time before 25 October, he had been telling his wife about "them" – he never defined "them" – who were trying to get him. He spoke of "them" again that night, just before leaping out of his chair.

After he left the house he went to a bar, but before he could take even his first sip of the beer he had ordered, he collapsed unconscious. Witnesses say he was sober and was not slurring either before or after he passed out. When he came round, he drove off.

At 1 a.m., he turned up in the village where he had grown up, knocking on the door of a woman he had known since childhood, who had not seen him since. He kept saying there had been a "horrible incident". The woman told him it was too late to talk and he should go to his parents'. He drove off, leaving the woman scared and baffled.

At 3 a.m. his car was found by two truck drivers, crashed in a trench by the side of the A45 road, 60 miles from where he had last been seen.

The truck drivers reported that Günther Stoll was still conscious – and stark naked. Curiously, he was sitting in the front passenger seat. They also claimed they saw what seemed to be an injured man in white walking away in the distance. One tried to catch up to him but failed.

Stoll told the men that there had been four men in the car, who had all run away. They asked him if the four men were his friends. "No," he replied. It was the last thing he ever said.

Who were the men? Were they "them"? Was the injured man one of "them"? Where did he go?

The police investigation revealed more troubling details about Stoll's misfortune. He had not died in a car crash, it was revealed. His injuries proved he had been run down by a car in a separate incident, and then his naked body moved to the passenger seat of his own car. Why? And by whom? Police drew a blank.

Lots of theories have been put forward about YOG'TZE. Was it a number plate which Stoll had a premonition of being hit by? No car with this plate has ever been located, nor has a plate with "YO6'TZE" on it, as some think the note might have said. When the note was turned upside down the handwriting seemed to read "027,906". Did Stoll deliberately write upside down as a sort of cipher?

It is a mystery that Günther Stoll has taken to the grave with him.

MYTHICAL
CREATURES

Type, species, genus. It has been one of the great achievements of science to study and catalogue the animals of the Earth and the birds of the sky and classify them by type. But as any scientist will tell you, despite all the progress, we have just scraped the surface.

Maybe even less than that. For what of the unique, hidden and secret creatures which have inhabited the world since Eve met her talking snake? This is the realm of the cryptozoologist, and what they hunt are cryptids, those fantastic beasts which populate the places science can't get to: folklore, dreams, caves and deep beneath the ocean.

Most famous among them are the Loch Ness Monster and Big Foot, but these need no introduction. They are just two of the millions of creatures whose existence is claimed, disputed, claimed again and disputed again. Elders speak of them, and people track them, and their trail might go cold for a century or two before their hibernation is done.

The world of the cryptozoologist is the endless search for these beasts, and the triumph of writing in the catalogue "former cryptid", such as the cyclops shark, the Polish mountain lion, the sabretooth deer and Hogzilla, which have now found to be real animals. Scientists laughed at cryptozoologists who proposed the existence of these astonishing creatures; now cryptozoologists laugh back like an Indonesian Cehehe.

So let's take a journey into jungles and deserts, up mountains and down into the oceans, and remember that all animals were once cryptids, and all of these will be until suddenly they are not.

CHUPACABRA

The village of Moca in Puerto Rico has always been best known for its handmade lace, Mundillo. But in 1975 it drew attention for an entirely different reason. A number of local farmers noticed they were losing livestock, particularly goats, in a peculiar fashion. The goats weren't missing, they were being found dead. Their bodies were bled dry and they had circular incisions. At first it was thought that they were being used by satanists, although some said vampires – *el vampiro de Moca*. Soon after the killings stopped, and Moca returned to making lace.

Then in 1995, the killings resumed in a nearby town. Goats, sheep and other domestic animals were found dead, again drained of blood. This time there could, according to wise locals, be no doubt. This was the work of Chupacabra (*chupar*, "to suck", and *cabra*, "goat") – the legendary "goat suckers" of Puerto Rico. Eyewitness Madelyne Tolentino described a creature that stood upright, four to five feet tall with spikes down its back, long, thin arms and legs, and an alien-like oblong head. It resembled, she said, a reptilian kangaroo with huge red eyes. Hundreds of Puerto Rican animals had reputedly fallen victim to the Chupacabra's desire for blood.

Soon, animals across North and South America were succumbing to the Chupacabra. Sightings grew more frequent. As far away as India, the Chupacabra was spotted savaging chickens, in addition to goats and sheep. Humans were at least spared the Chupacabra's attentions – but how will its tastes develop in the future?

In 2007, a rancher in Elmendorf, Texas got tired of losing his livestock to these creatures and waited with his gun. He saw a hairless beast roaming his fields. He shot it and took it in to be examined.

DNA testing suggested that it was a coyote with mange, but if so, how to explain the strange circumstances of the livestock deaths? And if this *was* a coyote, that doesn't show that all Chupacabra are coyotes – there are no coyotes in India.

More Chupacabra have been found in Texas since – on golf courses and ditches, near farms and on ranches. One found in Blanco, Texas is now in a museum, the mystery of its provenance unsolved. Could these Chupacabra be, as some have suggested, either aliens or the pets of aliens? How else to explain their sudden arrival? Or are they a species of terrestrial bat – the areas where they are found are famous for vampire bats. Could this be a bat that science has yet to identify, or that has crossed the species divide with some sort of canine?

In the last few years, the number of sightings has died down, and the amount of animals found dead with their blood sucked out has also fallen. But as anyone will tell you, cryptid time is not the same as human time, so what seems a long while to us might seem the blink of an eye to them. After all, it was 20 years between the first sighting and the second. Is that the gestation period of a Chupacabra? Could a new generation of this beast be preparing to terrorize the poor farm animals of the Americas?

MATTHEW AND THE MERMAID

On the south coast of England, in a Cornish village called Zennor, there is a beautiful story told. In the local church the tiny population were occasionally joined on a Sunday by a beautiful woman. At the end of the service she would slip away before anyone could ask her who she was or where she came from. No matter how many years passed between visits, she never seemed to age and her bell-like voice still rang as exquisitely when she sang as it always had.

One day in the fifteenth century, to the village churchwarden's wife was born a boy named Matthew Trewella. As he grew it became clear that he too had a wondrous voice. The beautiful stranger had not been seen for many years, but on Matthew Trewella's eighteenth birthday, there she was, in the pew opposite him.

As the first hymn began, the voices of Matthew and the stranger rose above the others and became entwined. The other parishioners fell silent and listened to the glorious singing. This happened as each hymn was sung, and by the final "Hallelujah" no one else dared make a sound.

At the end of the service, the beautiful stranger slipped

away as she always had, but Matthew, inflamed by her beauty and her song, followed quickly after. The villagers watched from the summit of Tregarthen Hill, as down below he chased her across the fields towards the rough Cornish sea. The pair disappeared around a final bend, never to be seen again.

Zennor folk believe the woman was a mermaid, and that she and Matthew found love in the foaming brine. A while later, they had a mermaid carved into the end of the pew in which the stranger sat, in case she ever returned to Zennor. One can see it to this day. Does she keep away because Matthew still lives with her beneath the sea, or is she waiting for another man with a voice as sweet as his?

All that can be said for certain is that many years later a sea captain claims to have seen the Mermaid of Zennor again. One Sunday morning he weighed anchor at nearby Pendower Cove. While smoking his pipe on deck, he heard the most lovely voice singing. Looking into the water, he saw a beautiful mermaid with long flowing hair.

She asked if he could raise his anchor, as it was blocking the door of her home beneath the sea. She was anxious to get back to her husband Matthew and their children. The captain did so, and before she dived asked her name. "Morveren," said the mermaid, and the captain recognized her as one of the daughters of Llyr, King of the Ocean.

She is not the only mermaid to make the Cornish seas her home. Not far away at Padstow is a sandbar at the head of the estuary, named Doom Bar, for all the ships run aground there. They say that it was formed by another mermaid, who was shot by local man Tristram Bird. He saw a stunning woman upon the rocks and asked her to marry him. When she refused he shot her. As she died, she cursed the ground on which he stood. Next day the Doom Bar was there.

Tristram Bird, however, was not.

THE MINOTAUR

The Greek myths have given us some of the most memorable fantastical creatures of all time, but perhaps none rouse such passion, anger and sadness as the Minotaur. Born half-human half-bull, he devoured men for his sustenance.

His mother was Pasiphae, the wife of King Minos of Crete. Minos wished to see if the gods preferred him to his brothers, and asked Poseidon, the sea deity, to send him a snow-white bull to show he was the favourite. In return Minos would slaughter the bull.

But the bull was so beautiful Minos decided to keep him. As revenge, Poseidon ordered the master craftsman Daedalus to fashion a wooden cow, into which he placed Pasiphae. The union of her and the bull produced the Minotaur.

In his anger and jealousy, Minos asked Daedalus to imprison the Minotaur. Knowing that the enormous strength and powerful jaws of the Minotaur would allow him to break through any prison he might build, Daedalus created a maze which he named "Labyrinth" to hold the creature. But still Crete shook with his awful bellowing, and however ingenious the Labyrinth, Minos still feared that the Minotaur would escape.

In the meantime, he won a war against Athens. He ordered that every year hence the seven bravest Athenian men and seven most beautiful Athenian women be handed to him to sacrifice. Perhaps they died to the sound of the Minotaur's bellowing?

In the third year, a young Athenian named Theseus – the son of King Aegeus of Athens – offered to kill the Minotaur in exchange for ending the sacrifices. He travelled to Crete by ship, telling his father it would return under a white sail if he had succeeded, a black sail if he had failed.

On seeing the handsome Theseus, Ariadne, the daughter of King Minos, fell instantly in love, and, on the advice of Daedalus, gave the hero a ball of thread so he could find his way out of the Labyrinth. Tying the thread to a doorhandle, Theseus entered the Labyrinth.

Accounts vary about what happened between Theseus and the Minotaur. Some say the Minotaur was sleeping at the heart of the Labyrinth, others that he was exhausted from roaming around and bellowing for his freedom. It is agreed that Theseus slew the Minotaur, stabbing the half-human half-bull in the throat and decapitating him.

Retracing his steps using Ariadne's thread, Theseus was able to free all of the Athenians and take them to the ship. Ariadne came with him, as did her sister, Phaedra. So bewitched was Theseus with these daughters of Minos, he forgot to raise the white sail, and so his father thought he was dead and killed himself by leaping into the sea, known as the Aegean Sea to this day.

And what of the Minotaur? There are some who call this the saddest of stories – like Frankenstein's monster, he did not choose his birth. They say he only fed on men because there is no natural food for a creature that was made rather than that evolved. They say that some quiet nights in Crete you can still hear the bellowing of the Minotaur in his Labyrinth, or the sound of Pasiphae weeping for the child she nursed.

THE GORGONS

If the tale of the Minotaur can evoke sorrow, the tale of the Gorgons evokes nothing but terror. Originally, none of the Greek poets could say precisely what a Gorgon looked like, perhaps as no one who had seen one lived to tell the tale. Some thought they had claws and wings, others that they had tusks. What was agreed was that they were closer to reptiles than to humans, and that they only meant harm to humans.

It was only later that the Greeks came to understand the Gorgons, and to know that they were three sisters, Stheno, Euryale and Medusa, and that they had snakes on their heads instead of hair, and a single glance at them would turn you to stone. It was Medusa who caused the most havoc – being mortal unlike her sisters, her anger was the greatest, and her victim tally the highest.

Some say that she was born mortal and turned into a Gorgon by the goddess Athena after she saw Medusa making love to Poseidon in one of her temples. As Poseidon had been aroused by Medusa's flowing locks, Athena turned them into snakes so no man, let alone god, could be with her again. Anyone would be angry about that!

It was Perseus, legend has it, who slew Medusa and ended her reign of terror. Armed only with a scythe, he approached the Gorgon with his eyes averted. When he was close enough, he did not look at her as others had done before, nor did he reach for her blindly as some fools had, to be bitten by her snakes.

Instead he looked at the reflection of Medusa in his mirrored shield – gifted to him by Athena – and landed a blow upon her neck, killing her instantly, and then keeping the severed head in a sack. Some say each drop of blood became a snake, and each snake on Earth now is a descendent of Medusa, and may one day return to their queen or another they find worthy.

Some say that a few of the drops of blood flowed all the way to the sea and Poseidon mingled them with the salt water and foam to make Pegasus, the winged stallion, and his brother Chrysaor. Pegasus reputedly carries thunderbolts for Zeus, which is why it is said that snakes are especially active during storms. If you see one during such weather, stay well away, for a lightning bolt can allegedly return the snake to a Gorgon form.

After Perseus returned home from slaying Medusa, he had many adventures. He would use Medusa's severed head to turn his enemies to stone, including the horrifying sea monster Keto. On his return, Athena, who still held a grudge against Medusa, had the head incorporated into her own shield. As the goddess of feminine order she had tamed the wild power of Medusa, and it was believed this meant that all women would now refrain from indulging in the passions that Medusa found pleasure in...

Medusa herself was depicted thousands of times in Greek art, her face thought to ward off evil spirits. Some also believed that the blood from the right side of a Gorgon had healing powers, while blood from the left side brought instant death.

So if you do happen upon a Gorgon, don't look too closely, and ensure you know your left from your right...

THE ROUGAROU

If you find yourself in Louisiana, particularly near a swamp or bayou at night, you may want to make sure you are not alone.

During foggy nights in such places the Rougarou is said to appear. You might get some warning beforehand – the sound of growling, the snapping of twigs – but by then it will be too late. The Rougarou, with the head of a wolf and the body of a man, is fast and can run on two legs or four. Its bloodshot eyes are looking for only one thing: human blood.

Why Louisiana? This is the historically French part of the United States – named for the "Sun King", Louis XIV of France. It was in France that the creature first made its home, being known there as *Loup-garou* – which translates roughly as "werewolf". Perhaps the Rougarou travelled across the seas in the boats that took the settlers to America, secreted in the depths of their hulls.

In France the beasts were pious, for it is said they preyed only on children who ignored the rules of Lent or who were seen to misbehave. Parents tried to warn their kids about the Loup-garou, but still some ended up taken away. Legend has it that those who break Lent seven years in a row turn into Loup-garou, after which they automatically change their form. Perhaps these people had a taste for human blood all along?

The Rougarou of Louisiana are less choosy about their victims, although Cajun legend still has it that breaking the rules of Lent remains most provocative. Indeed, allegedly simply looking at a Rougarou is enough to turn a person into one, leaving them wandering the swamplands. The curse supposedly only lasts 101 days. After that it is transferred to another human, who must also seek blood until the curse lifts.

Some embrace the legend of the Rougarou – there is a festival held each year in the village of Houma, where the locals elect a queen and dress as the monster and dance. Eerily there always seem to be more Rougarou there than tickets sold. And fewer villagers after the event.

Others believe that the Rougarou is a creation of witchcraft. As everyone knows, witches are notorious for their experiments in lycanthropy – the making of werewolves. Might the use of the herb wolfbane see them off, as it was said to in medieval Europe? Or could they be vanquished simply by saying their Christian name three times, as they swear by in parts of Germany? Or, as the ancient Greeks believed, is the power of exhaustion sufficient? Greek werewolves were forced to carry out physical activities for hours on end, to cure them of their malady.

But if you do find yourself living down by the bayou, and the nights are growing foggy, and the moon is getting full, there is one simple solution to keep the Rougarou away. All you need to do is place 13 objects outside your door. Legend has it that the Rougarou can only count to 12, and when they try and see how many objects there are they get confused and angry and leave the house in peace.

Or, of course, you could always follow the rules of Lent, and make sure you do as your parents tell you.

HAFGUFA

Seventy per cent of the Earth's surface is water, and the average depth is about 2.5 miles. But some areas go much deeper, as deep as 7 miles. Most organisms we know of live very near the ocean's surface. There is almost no sunlight after the first half a mile, barely a tenth of the way down.

In fact, 95 per cent of the Earth's living space is beneath the ocean. What creatures are down there? And do they ever emerge?

Many have spoken of the Kraken, a giant octopus, which is said to sink ships with its massive tentacles. Hans Egde, in the eighteenth century, wrote a book about sea serpents and giant crabs, as they had been witnessed by Norwegian sailors over many years. The Kraken was many miles long, "having many heads and a number of claws". Only by pronouncing its name could you escape its clutches once caught.

But even the Kraken, they say, is dwarfed by the Hafgufa of Icelandic legend. First identified in the thirteenth century, Hafgufa can reputedly eat whole ships and whales. In the Icelandic legend *The King's Mirror*, a king reports that of all the whales that inhabit the seas, it is the Hafgufa one must fear.

The size of an island, the Hafgufa would lie still for long periods, hiding from man. Then, when hungry, the Hafgufa would vomit out a previous meal to entice fish or larger prey. When you see many fish gathered, it may be the Hafgufa drawing you in. According to the king, the Hafgufa is infertile, as only two have ever been seen – the same two for thousands of years.

It was these two that the legendary hero Örvar-Oddr encountered as he sailed the fjords of Helluland. Coming to an island, five of his crew disembarked, only to find themselves in the grip of a Hafgufa. Though those souls were lost, the feasting of the Hafgufa allowed Örvar-Oddr to sail past and on to safety.

And could it be on the Hafgufa's back that St Brendan the Navigator preached a Mass on his journey to the Isle of the Blessed in 512 CE? Searching for the Garden of Eden, St Brendan and his men stopped on an island to celebrate Easter and lit a fire to warm themselves. The island soon revealed itself to be a giant fish, and they were forced to run to their ship. The saint knew this fish as "Jasconius", mentioned in ancient Greek texts, and believed it to be the one that swallowed Jonah in the Bible story of Jonah and the Whale.

There have been fewer sightings of the Hafgufa in recent years; perhaps there were only ever two, perhaps they have all gone. But these were still creatures of the light, of the small surface of the ocean which comes into contact with human beings. Could it be that deeper in the ocean, in the places where light never penetrates, there are creatures that dwarf even the Hafgufa? And could it be that only a tiny change in the world might draw them up towards the surface, slowly, slowly but inevitably? Might it be that the next ship that sinks in weird circumstances may have once again encountered a fantastic beast, hungry for something new and increasingly plentiful?

AKKOROKAMUI

If you find yourself looking for the Hafgufa, you may want to take a detour to Funka Bay in Hokkaidō, where you may be lucky enough to see a creature that first made itself known in the Shinto folklore of Japan.

Part human, part octopus, Akkorokamui is also sometimes called Ashketanne Mat, the Long-fingered Woman. Its red hue is "likened to the colour of the reflection of the setting sun upon water". It is known as a creature of healing and able to bestow knowledge. When you visit a shrine to Akkorokamui, you must wash your hands and then deliver fish, crabs and molluscs, and you will then be granted good health.

Moreover, Akkorokamui is known to be able to grow back lost limbs and is particularly good on broken arms and other limb injuries.

But take care, as Akkorokamui can be fickle and you don't want to get on its bad side or it won't just grab you in one of its inescapable tentacles, but, in its own words, "I shall swallow the whale and ship, empty the sea, and appear in red when you are cursed."

You have been warned.

THE BANSHEE

It's the screaming that gets to you first. Then the wailing, the howling, the shrieking. Sometimes the screaming takes on the sound of a lament – this is called keening. A family member has died somewhere, either close to home or far away, or you yourself are approaching the end, and the banshee has arrived. No one knows if she is a fairy or a ghost, and there are many who claim she was murdered or died in childbirth. To hear her may bring comfort, or it may portend death.

Some have described her perching on a windowsill in avian form, like the Devil Bird of Sri Lanka, only assuming human form in the hours before death, sometimes with flaming red hair and a white dress, sometimes with a grey cloak and green dress.

Whatever she wears, her complexion is always spectral and her eyes red from crying. She lives in grief and comes to share it.

Some say she only visits noble families, but she has been seen near paupers' homes, crouching beneath trees, weeping bitterly. Or assuming the looks of a young relative and keening in the moonlight. On sight she may disappear in the mist, or take wing and soar into the night. Others say she can assume many forms, like the weasel, the stoat or the hooded crow.

162

The banshees' queen is said to be Clíodhna, a goddess of beauty and love, whose three birds sing so sweetly they can cure the sickest mortal. But it is not the place of banshees to either cause or prevent the deaths of mortals. They are there to guide and to mourn.

Perhaps there are as many banshees as there are families. Some say that every family has a banshee spirit, which is always there beside them, and only as death approaches does she begin to wail. If you don't hear her but find a silver comb on the ground, she may have been there and then fled, and the end may be coming soon.

Legend also has it that when many banshees appear it means the demise of someone important, and kings, queens and heads of the family should be forewarned that the lamentation means they are about to make their final journey.

One of the oldest and best-known accounts of an encounter with a banshee is that of the English diarist and recipe writer Lady Fanshawe. In 1642, she and her husband Sir Richard were staying at a baronial castle when she was woken in the night by a scream. "Then she beheld in the moonlight a female face and part of her figure hovering at the window. The apparition continued to exhibit itself for some time, and then vanished with two shrieks similar to that which she heard at first."

The following morning she reported the unnatural encounter to her host, who replied without emotion or fear, "What my dear Lady Fanshawe had witnessed and heard was a banshee and her wailing forecast of death came true as a near relation of my family expired last night in the castle."

So if you hear the shriek of the banshee you may be in noble company. But not, alas, for long.

MONGOLIAN DEATH WORM

"It is shaped like a sausage about two feet long, has no head nor leg and it is so poisonous that merely to touch it means instant death. It lives in the most desolate parts of the Gobi Desert."

So said Mongolian Prime Minister Damdinbazar in 1922. He was speaking of the Mongolian death worm, called "olgoi-khorkhoi" by the local population. Rarely seen and never photographed – to encounter one is usually to die – it has been credited with a great many methods of killing. By all accounts, it can spit corrosive venom over great distances, burning the flesh away from the bone completely. Or it can electrocute, either by touch or by sending out a charge as someone or something approaches.

Its flesh may be pink or red and some have described a spike coming out of each end, which is how it shoots its poison or electrical charges. Like so much in the Mongolian desert, it acts silently – you are dead before you realize it is there. It is said to hibernate for ten months a year, only emerging in rainy June and July.

The American palaeontologist Roy Chapman Andrews – believed to be the model for Indiana Jones – first tried to chronicle the existence of the worm in 1926 while searching for dinosaur eggs. No one Andrews spoke to had seen the creature "but they all firmly believed in its existence and described it minutely," he wrote.

Since then the worm has been elusive, partly because it allegedly travels underground – some speculate that the waves on the Mongolian sands are caused by it moving under the surface. Woe betide anyone who steps on one of the ripples...

It is not just humans who should be wary. Legend has it that the Mongolian death worm is quite partial to camels. Not only does it kill them for food, but it lays its eggs in the large intestine, where they hatch, burrowing their way back out and into the desert sand. One can always tell a camel which has played host to olgoi-khorkhoi – they have been turned the same shade of red as the worm itself.

A number of explorers have scoured the Gobi Desert looking for the worm. Some have even tried to "thump" it out of the ground as is done with earthworms – the ancient art of "worm charming" or "worm grunting" – but without success. According to locals interviewed for a television show in 2009, sightings peaked in the 1950s. But as the Gobi Desert has been investigated more thoroughly, sightings have gone down. "The worm has fled," the interviewees said.

But maybe it has just continued on its journey across the Gobi. The desert is, after all, over 500,000 square miles of rough terrain, and if a creature, even one as big as olgoi-khorkhoi, chose to hide, there are plenty of places it can go. As Prime Minister Damdinbazar said, it is in the desolate corners of the desert where the worm prefers to dwell. As long as the odd human passes by, and the odd camel is available as a breeding ground, the giant worm has no need for anything else, and certainly not publicity or scientists poking their noses in.

GROOTSLANG

The story goes that the gods made a mistake when they created Grootslangs, with their long scaly bodies, huge heads and tusks. Reportedly they are huge, but they also have too much strength, cunning and intelligence, so no other creature near them will be safe. Legends say that the gods decided to split the Grootslangs in two, and thus were born both elephants and snakes.

But one escaped before it could be sundered. From this one, more Grootslangs were born. Still angry, they are thought to lure elephants into their cave and eat them as revenge for the acts of the gods.

They are said to dwell in a cave called the Wonder Hole in the Richtersveld desert of South Africa. Supposedly, the cave leads to a 40-mile underground channel filled with diamonds. The Grootslang's lust for diamonds is insatiable; should you encounter one, make sure you have a handful to give it. There are even those who say that the Grootslang's love of diamonds is so great that its eyes are now a pair of them, flashing at its latest victim.

They will also tell you of the English businessman Peter Grayson, who in 1917 went searching for treasures in Richtersveld. Members of his party saw him approaching the Wonder Hole, his eyes glinting as greedily as a Grootslang's.

No sooner had he peered into the hole than they heard the crunching of bones and saw nothing but his boots in the air, as he descended one chomp at a time.

Some say the Grootslang will not die until it has stashed in its lair every diamond in the world...

THE WOLPERTINGER

If there's one thing which unites most cryptids, it is that they are terrifying, dangerous and threatening. But sometimes they are none of these things. Could a cryptid be... cute?

If you visit the forests of Bavaria, Germany, where people still dress in traditional clothing such as *lederhosen*, dance around the maypole and participate in whip-cracking competitions, you may be lucky enough to come across one of the most unusual of all the cryptids – the mythical Wolpertinger.

Also known as the Wolperdinger, Woibbadinga or Volpertinger, depending on which part of Bavaria you are from, this zany creature combines the body of a hare and the horns of a deer. It is said that one Bavarian night a hare and a deer fell in love, and the Wolpertinger was born. Later Wolpertingers are also thought to feature wings, tails and fangs, but many argue these are not the true Wolpertingers.

Wolpertingers are, they say, not dangerous to humans, although if its saliva touches your skin tufts of hair may grow. Also, despite its gentle nature, when cornered, the Wolpertinger can panic and spray you with a foul-smelling liquid, as a skunk can. No matter how much you scrub, the smell will not go until it is ready, which may take days or weeks. Enjoy its absence while you can – legend has it that the smell returns every seven years for the rest of your life.

Fortunately, the Wolpertinger is shy, and it is rare to see one in the wild. But there are ways to tempt it out of its hiding place. Locals say you should go into the forest on a full moon with the one you wish to marry or the one you are married to already – if you are with the right person, the Wolpertinger will emerge to give its blessing. Would you take the risk?

You can also use the "sack, stick, spade" method. Prop a sack open with a spade and place a lit candlestick inside. The Wolpertinger will be attracted to the light and go inside the sack. Pull the spade away quickly and you can trap the Wolpertinger within. Why it has to be a spade is unclear – perhaps to beat away anyone who tries to steal your valuable prize.

They also say that if you see one in the wild, you can drop salt on its tail, which makes it immobile. But as anyone will tell you, your chances of seeing a live one while carrying a salt shaker are vanishingly small.

It seems that the existence of the Wolpertinger has not only enchanted humans – other animals of the forest have become involved and the love between species has flourished. There have been sightings of the offspring of foxes and ducks, pheasants and squirrels, lynx and bats. Go to any local taxidermist and they will sell you one of these hybrid creatures to take home with you, with a certificate of authenticity.

But the true collector will surely return home with a stuffed Wolpertinger, or at least some of the Wolpertinger merchandise which is available everywhere. Strangely, it seems that only tourists to the area buy themselves a Wolpertinger – perhaps the locals are too used to seeing the little creature when walking the Bavarian woodlands? Or perhaps they've already got one?

THE DREAM EATER

"To sleep, perchance to dream – ay, there's the rub: for in that sleep of death what dreams may come?"

What dreams indeed. As Shakespeare's Hamlet knows, we can never anticipate what dreams may come to us. Will they be happy? Or confusing? Will we remember the whole thing or just parts? When we lie down, we never know what will happen.

Worst of all, will we have nightmares? For some people, the night is a time of terrors, as sleep once again allows the horrors in, while others are only visited occasionally by the demons of the witching hours. But there is no one on Earth who has not been woken with a start in the middle of the night, perhaps even sitting bolt upright with a scream.

What if there was a creature that could save us from nightmares? The Japanese venerate just such a creature – Baku. Baku is also known as the "dream eater" and legend has it that if summoned correctly, it will devour a nightmare for you, and you will never have it again.

It is said that Baku was created by the gods with the parts which were left over from creating all the other animals. This explains its strange appearance – a bear's body, an elephant's trunk, a tiger's paws, the tail of an ox, and rhinoceros ears or eyes. Some say it is a relation of the Chinese chimera Mo, which is hunted for its pelt, and which is said to have magical powers and protect the wearer from evil spirits. But no one hunts the Baku.

To summon the Baku, Japanese children are told to call three times, "Baku-san, come eat my dream, Baku-san, come eat my dream, Baku-san, come eat my dream" and the Baku will relieve them of their terrors and allow them to sleep in peace.

For this reason, images of the Baku have become talismans to ward off bad dreams – placed around your bed or that of your child, they are believed to stop the nightmares coming. Some people even sleep with an image of Baku beneath their pillow, or call to him for protection before they sleep. Some Japanese houses have shrines to Baku, and it is believed that no bad dreams ever enter, and those who live there are always fresh-faced and full of life.

But beware! Summoning Baku requires some caution. It is said that if you summon him too often, or if your nightmare is too small and he remains hungry after devouring it, then he may move on to gobble up your hopes and desires as well. If this happens, you will be fated to live an empty and unfulfilled life. You can see those who have summoned Baku frivolously – they live their lives listlessly and never dream of the future.

So Baku should only be summoned to deal with your biggest nightmares, to ensure that his belly is full by the time he is done. That way you will wake feeling happy and refreshed, and full of hopes and desires.

Repeat after me, "Baku-san, come eat my dream, Baku-san, come eat my dream, Baku-san, come eat my dream."

ORIGIN ENIGMATIC

In 1904, French Baron Maurice de Rothschild and zoologist Henri Neuville were visiting ivory markets in Ethiopia when they noticed a very odd-looking tusk on a stall owned by Indian merchants. While it resembled an elephant's tusk, it was much smaller. It was dark and had grooves running along its length, narrow on the outside of its curve, broad on the inside.

Rothschild and Neuville were able to purchase the tusk cheaply. Locals told them they thought it was the horn of a giant aquatic, hippopotamus-sized creature that dwelt in the lakes of East Africa. The pair were keen to get it home and study it properly.

They displayed it in Paris and London. Experts in the field drew a blank. The pair then wrote a scientific paper that labelled it *"d'origine énigmatique"* – origin enigmatic. The paper compared the bizarre item with the tusks of elephants, rhinoceroses and boars. It was different to all of them.

Try as they might, the pair could find no trace of any creature that might be the owner of such a tusk, either living or dead. Had the merchants been right, that there was a giant aquatic, hippopotamus-sized creature? Neither were in a position to go and find out, so they deposited the tusk in France's National Museum of Natural History in Paris.

MYTHICAL CREATURES

Despite being catalogued and filed, the tusk subsequently vanished forever. Many have tried to search for it in the markets of Ethiopia, the lakes of East Africa and the basement of the National Museum in Paris, with no luck.

Its disappearance has been as enigmatic as its origin.

SIGBINS

You are in the Philippines, walking your dog. You are holding your child's hand. Suddenly the dog starts running around and barking, and your child screams in horror. You look everywhere but see nothing. But neither your pet nor your child will calm down.

Overactive imaginations? Maybe. But maybe they can see what you cannot: a sigbin.

Legend has it that only the innocent eyes of children can see a sigbin – their eyes have not been sullied by the cruelty of the world like those of adults. To adults, the sigbin is invisible – except if they have a desire to terrify you, in which case they make themselves visible.

They can, however, be smelt, as they give off a nauseating odour. For this reason they tend to hide in places that disguise their smell, in cesspits, near livestock or in swamps. If these places make you retch, beware, for a sigbin might be adding his odour to the powerful stench.

Some say a sigbin looks like a dog, others that it recalls a goat. It walks on hind legs and has a long tail which can be used as a whip. Its feet are on the wrong way round, and so it walks backwards, with its head lowered between its hind legs. It also has long ears which it can clap together. Some believe it is related to the kangaroo.

The sigbin is most active during Holy Week, when it steals children's hearts and turns them into amulets. But adults are not safe either, for sigbins need human blood to survive. Unlike vampires, though, sigbins initially bite into the neck of a person's shadow, drawing the blood out that way.

You may not even know you have a sigbin attached, until you start to feel fatigued or incredibly tired. If you feel as though you are going to faint, it could well be that a sigbin is drinking from you. When you lie down to rest, the sigbin will reveal itself and go directly to the source.

But despite how dangerous they are – or maybe because of how dangerous they are – there are some who hunt the sigbin. These are the sigbinians, and they are said to keep their captives in jars of clay. Sigbinians either have or have developed the power to command the sigbins, and there are those who say that a sigbin attack is seldom random. If you have unknowingly crossed a sigbinian, or if they just think your blood might satisfy their terrible pets, you may expect to begin to feel fatigued for no reason at all.

It is also believed that the most frightening of Filipino creatures, the aswang – a shape-shifter that can appear as a vampire, a weredog or a ghoul – also keep sigbins, although aswangs also feed on humans. No one has ever been in a position to question this, however – one does not ask an aswang why they keep as companions fellow bloodsuckers.

But just remember, the next time your child tells you they see a monster, don't dismiss them so easily. And get as quickly as possible to a place where there are no shadows, or you might be overtaken by a terrible tiredness…

THE FROGMAN OF LOVELAND

May 1955. A businessman was driving through Loveland, Ohio, at 3.30 a.m., when he saw a curious sight. There beside the road, under a poorly lit bridge, the businessman saw three figures three to four feet tall, one of them waving a sparkler. Children, he thought, although it seemed weird they were out so late. But as he drove closer he realized with horror these were no children. They had leathery skin and the faces of frogs. Shaken, the businessman drove off as fast as he could.

Fast forward 17 years, to 1972. Ohio police officer Ray Shockey was driving through Loveland when a creature scurried in front of his car. Clearly illuminated in his car headlights was a creature three to four feet tall, with leathery skin and the face of a frog. It crouched in front of the car for a moment, then leapt the guardrail and was gone.

So was born the legend of the poetically named Frogman of Loveland. Over time, more and more sightings have occurred – the most recent in August 2016. Two children were playing Pokémon Go and found themselves at the very spot where Officer Shockey had seen his creature. There stood a giant frog, which raised itself onto its hind legs as the boys approached, before disappearing into the lake.

Before that in 1985, two other boys had a similar encounter.

In each case those that have seen the creature have provided the same description – the leathery skin, the frog face. Could this be a missing link between the reptile and the human? Or could it be an alien, lost on Earth with no way of getting home?

Whatever the creature is, no one in Loveland denies its existence. It has become something of a local celebrity with "I saw the Loveland Frog" T-shirts and a video game based on the beasts – even a musical, *Hot Damn! It's the Loveland Frog!*, which sets the tale of the Loveland Frogman to bluegrass music.

But is the Frogman unique to Loveland? In 1993, there were reports of a creature fitting the same description in Pretare d'Arquata in Italy, while in 1996, in Varginha, Brazil, two frogmen were seen by around 80 people and captured. The doctor who examined their bodies found that they had reptilian skin, three bony protuberances on their heads, long, forked tongues and claws on their feet. The policeman who captured them died soon after of a bacterial infection. Harmless as these creatures seem, perhaps it's best not to touch them.

Could these creatures be related to the Loveland Frogman? Could it even be that they are one and the same? Sightings have been sporadic, and we know nothing about how well it can travel, so it is not beyond the bounds of possibility…

Some claim these sightings are a hoax, or that there is no Loveland Frogman – just an escaped iguana, perhaps. But we can also point to the Goliath Frog of Cameroon, once thought to be mythical but then found very much alive and real. At 33 cm wide and weighing over 3 kg, it dwarfs other frogs. If one frog can grow so big, then there may be no limits.

And maybe one day the Frogman of Loveland will be defined in the same way as the Goliath Frog – "former cryptid".

THE AWFUL

Sometimes words fail even experienced cryptozoologists. For every "Bare Fronted Hoodwink" or "Nayarit Ruffed Cat" or "Jumpin' Yuccy", there is a beast about which nothing can be said except "Nameless Thing of Berkeley Square", "Unknown Norwegian Creature" or "Abominable Swamp Slob". Perhaps the most awful of these creatures is, well, "The Awful".

It was long thought that The Awful was not only a footnote to cryptid history, but to literary history. The horror writer H. P. Lovecraft is thought to have based some of his stories on the legend of The Awful. Lovecraft went so far as to visit the place where it was allegedly first seen, Richford and Berkshire in Vermont, USA.

It was here, in 1925, that some sawmill workers were crossing a bridge in the middle of town and saw what they thought was a bird of prey glaring down at them from a rooftop. As they approached, they saw that this was like no bird they had seen before. For a start it was huge – its grey wings, which it spread menacingly at them, had a wingspan of over 20 feet, while its tail was as long as its wings were wide. It also had giant claws, which one of the men later said "could easily grip a milk can's girth".

It was, as they said, "awful" – so awful that one of the men had a heart attack there and then, and for weeks the others would awake in the night screaming. Over the next few weeks, The Awful circled the town, landing on rooftops and staring at the petrified population as they tried to go about their chores. Some claimed they had seen a baby in its talons, others that it was taking livestock, but no one wanted to get close enough to check.

Oella Hopkins was hanging out washing when her dog became agitated, running around the yard and barking. Oella pulled aside the sheets and there it was, sitting on the roof of her farmhouse, staring at her angrily. She grabbed her dog and ran inside, hiding under the bed for hours.

No doubt many of the townsfolk tried to think of another name for this malevolent griffin-like creature, but no other name ever described it as precisely as the original. When it left, the relief of the local population could be felt miles away. For a long time it was believed The Awful would never return, or even that it was a folk tale told by grandparents to scare their grandchildren.

Then, in 2006, there was an article in the local newspaper about a well-respected member of the community who had seen a griffin-like creature swoop down and pluck a crow from a tree. Soon after another local said she had been sitting by Trout River when she saw a creature which looked like a pterodactyl staring at her. Other townsfolk backed up their claims, noting that the creature had such giant wings that you could hear them flapping long before you saw The Awful itself.

Nobody really knows what The Awful wants, or where it goes when it's not in Vermont. Mothers and fathers always do a head count of their children round there, but as one man told a cryptozoologist on the hunt for The Awful, the locals have mostly learned to live with their mysterious visitor. As he put it, "We don't bother it and it don't bother us... maybe with a few exceptions."

XIEZHI

Whatever your crime, from a parking ticket to something more serious such as murder, there are few things as scary as standing before a judge.

But even if you are up for murder, it's worth remembering things could be worse. You could be appearing before Gao Yao, the minister for justice to the legendary Emperor Shun sometime between 2294 and 2184 BCE.

Gao Yao had a simple method for finding out if you were guilty or innocent. Its name was Xiezhi, which looked something like a single-horned ox, if the single-horned ox had body armour, a helmet of spikes and huge jaws. The accused was simply brought before Xiezhi. If he was innocent, Xiezhi would pay no mind. If they were guilty, Xiezhi would ram into them, pierce them with its horn, tear them to shreds and devour them. Whether one could take a small fine instead is not mentioned.

Statues of the Xiezhi still adorn law courts in China, Korea and Japan, although the creature himself seems to be extinct. It is said that one day King Xuan of Qi asked his minister Ai Zi about his statue of the Xiezhi outside of parliament. When it saw a corrupt politician, he said, it pierced him with its horn on the spot and devoured him. "If such an animal lived today," he added, "it would not need to go hungry."

THE BLACK STICK MEN

Cryptids have long held a fascination for graphic novelists, anime artists and the creators of virtual worlds. Because their sightings are so rare, artists are free to produce images that can be overpowering in their complexity and detail. But what if there was a creature that not only looked like an illustration to begin with, but the simplest possible illustration? So it is with a species which have been sighted more and more often in recent years – the Black Stick Men.

Like The Awful, the clue to their appearance is in the name. These enigmatic beings look like humanoid stick figures and lack any facial features – no eyes, nose or mouth. They range from normal human proportions to many feet tall. While assumed to be male, no gender can be established. They are black from head to toe, and some speculate they are two-dimensional beings in our three-dimensional world – meaning that they appear exactly the same from any angle. They have no shadow.

While no one who has seen a Black Stick Man has come to any harm, witnesses say they feel a great deal of agitation and even aggression when in the presence of one, almost like the beings are charged with electricity. Might Black Stick Men feed on negative energy, as experts say that Astral Vampires, which feed on human emotions, do? Or do the forces in their dimension differ to those in ours?

A young girl in Phoenix, Arizona, reported seeing a freaky sticklike figure walking backwards and forwards on the electrical wire across the road. She called her cousin to come and look, and she saw it too. Too frightened to tell their parents they ran back inside and hid. The girl tried to put it out of her mind – until she heard stories of the Black Stick Men and realized what she had seen...

In another account, a man in Essex, England, saw a black sticklike figure run across the road in front of him. The man is a nurse and not normally a believer in the paranormal or in cryptids. But he saw what he saw, and again it was only as sightings increased that he began to understand he was not alone. As with other encounters, the Essex stick figure left him feeling agitated. It was the same for a boy in nearby Kent. Even as an adult he gets angry when he tells the story of the Black Stick Man he saw in childhood, silhouetted against his wardrobe doors.

As the number of sightings has increased, researchers have speculated that these creatures are a new phenomenon, a sign that something has torn in the dimensions of our own universe. And yet... as some have pointed out, haven't these creatures appeared in pictures since the dawn of human existence? Scientists have long puzzled over why cave paintings of very sophisticated animals often have very rudimentary human figures beside them. Could it be that these are not images of the first hunters, but of the people who taught humans to hunt?

And perhaps drawing them is the only way forward. While cryptozoologists have tried to photograph them, a perfect image of them has remained elusive. How can one capture a two-dimensional figure on film?

Perhaps the cave men were onto something?

ETIÄINEN

Ever had a premonition of something about to occur which moments later does?

Well, that is probably just your Etiäinen going about its business, slightly ahead of you. According to Finnish folklore we each have one, a spirit of our own, existing just a little bit into the future.

How far ahead of us the Etiäinen lives is not clear. Some believe just a few seconds, finishing the next sentence to the one you are reading, or perhaps even more, onto the next tale. Some believe they can take some control over their Etiäinen and send them further ahead in time, and sense when they return whether it will be a good year or a bad one, but this takes tremendous energy and also risks losing your Etiäinen somewhere in the future. If it is far enough ahead to reach your death, you will live a spiritless life until you catch up with it...

But what if you are the Etiäinen of someone else? What would be different about what you are doing right now?

LET HER GO

It is usually the doe-like eyes that attract the man. She is wondrous in all other ways too, with high cheekbones, full lips and flowing hair. Her body is attractive, her smile radiant as anything. But in the end it is the eyes.

And so he follows her, leaving the campfire and going into the woods. She beckons him on; try as he might, he can not resist. In fact, he doesn't even try. Her beauty pulls him away from his friends and family, until he can no longer hear their voices.

They enter a clearing. The woman stops and turns to him. He gazes into those extraordinary eyes, runs his own eyes down her body, then takes in her breasts, hips, legs. And then he sees them. She doesn't have feet – she has hooves. It is the last thing he will ever see as he feels a kick to his chest. He falls on his back. Yet another man has been trampled by the shadowy Deer Woman.

They say that to those who respect women and children she is a bringer of fertility and love, and a protector from evil spirits. But to any man who has harmed women or children, she is vengeance itself and will lure them to their deaths. The eyes of a deer, yes, but also the hooves of a deer – hooves that can stomp a man into the grave.

MYTHICAL CREATURES

She appears in indigenous American mythology as a shape-shifter who is sometimes all-woman, sometimes all-deer and sometimes a hybrid of the two. She is, they say, fond of dancing and will join in any dance – whether you see her or not, you can hear the beating of her hooves.

Some compare her to the sirens of Greek mythology, who lured sailors to their deaths, or to the succubi, the demons who take men to bed and drain their energy. In some stories, she does not trample the man, instead enchanting him until he wastes away in his desperation to please her.

To some she is a symbol of female empowerment and transformation and will appear to any woman in need of protection or wisdom. What happens in these encounters is undocumented, for this is the business of the woman and the woman only. To tell the tale is to breach trust, and in the history of the Deer Woman this has never been done, no matter how many chroniclers have attempted to record the story.

If you are a man who has done wrong, you might try using tobacco leaves and chanting to keep the Deer Woman from your door, or you might be lucky enough to see her hooves before you are captured by her eyes. It is said that the Deer Woman will run away when recognized like this, although some claim she will allow you to make love to her, and you will become a better rider or warrior. But beware, if you do not satisfy her, she will drive you insane as revenge. In this way she protects the community, by doing away with useless men.

Or perhaps the answer is not to do wrong to women and children in the first place, or make amends when you have. Otherwise, it is said, the last thing you might see on Earth is a pair of hooves raining down on you in the dark.

ROADKILL

Some creatures appear numerous times in the literature of cryptozoology, in different forms, different places and different times. But sometimes a creature so unique appears that it threatens to overthrow everything we believe about not only cryptozoology, but zoology too.

On a hot day in 1996, Barbara Mullins was driving down Highway 12 in Louisiana when she saw a large creature dead on the roadside. Initially she thought it was a St Bernard dog. But as she approached it, she noticed something unusual. These were not the legs and feet of a dog. They were the legs and feet of a simian. The head and bald face were like a cross between a dog and an ape. The creature had a snub nose and small pointy ears, and was covered in brown hair, which was thicker than any dog hair she had seen. Whatever this was, it was no St Bernard.

Barbara had her camera with her and took a series of photographs of the bizarre beast, which she later submitted to the Louisiana Department of Wildlife and Fisheries. A long time passed before they came back with their verdict. It was nothing, they said, just a Pomeranian dog. But as Barbara pointed out, the Pomeranian is tiny, weighing only around seven pounds. This was the size of a St Bernard, closer to 300 pounds. And Pomeranians don't have ape-like heads or feet.

In the local area of DeRidder, Barbara's story became a talking point. The *DeQuincy News* published the photos. They thought it might be a Chupacabra – the "goat sucker", see page 146 – or even the voracious Devil Monkey, which has been spotted in Arizona and can leap 20 feet at a time, attacking domestic animals and the occasional human. Had this one leapt into the road and met its fate?

Further investigations turned up bones believed to belong to the creature, but these did appear to be purely canine. Besides, the creature was fully intact when Barbara Mullins found it on the roadside. It is one of the dangers of cryptozoology that individuals try and interfere with investigations with wild claims. These bones seem to have come from someone just wanting a piece of the action.

So what is it? It's possible, of course, that this is no cryptid, but a primate not previously found in the United States. This would be remarkable too and call into question some of the most firmly held beliefs in zoology.

Meanwhile, cryptozoologists continue to look for clues as to what this strange creature is, or was. Some have even said he or she is Rougarou, the Cajun werewolf (see page 157) – if so, it is no wonder this creature of the swamps became disorientated beside a busy motorway.

Barbara Mullins has disappeared, but her photographs have not. To this day the Louisiana Department of Wildlife and Fisheries is sticking to its story about the Pomeranian, and to this day cryptozoologists debate what the creature really is, among themselves and online. Perhaps one day the truth will out, and the moment Barbara Mullins aimed her camera and shot is the moment that humans found out for certain that the world is even stranger than they could possibly have imagined.

SHADOW CATS

One night in 2009, a woman in Allentown, Pennsylvania was sleeping peacefully when she felt her new cat leap onto the bed and climb onto her chest. Thinking it wanted to be comforted, she opened her eyes and said its name. What she saw horrified her. The cat's ears were pulled back, its fangs bared and it was snarling and spitting at her. As she tried to push it off, the cat clawed at her face.

A shadow loomed around it and the woman felt like she was suffocating. In desperation she called out, "Oh, God, save me from this evil!" The cat was thrown backwards, landed on its feet and fled the room, never to be seen again. When the woman confronted the people she'd bought the cat from they said they had rescued it from a couple who had been using it in satanic rituals. They suggested the cat was possessed.

If you type "animal possession" into an internet search engine, you'll find many videos and pictures of crazy-looking pets or of animals behaving in chaotic ways. You'll also find pet exorcism services. According to those in the know, animal possession is as possible as human possession. After all, according to the Bible, Jesus cast an evil spirit out of a man and into a herd of swine, causing them to run into a lake and kill themselves.

Some believe that cats are particularly susceptible to possession due to their long history as the familiars of witches. Others hold that when a cat sees a human for the first time they know immediately when and where that person will die, whether the cat is possessed or not. So they are a perfect vessel for malign spirits.

Sometimes there is no need for a malign spirit to take possession. Some Japanese believe that after a time all cats are transformed into *nekomata*, which gives them the power of necromancy, the ability to communicate with the dead. They can raise corpses and make them perform ritualistic dances. Nekomata can even taunt humans by calling up visions of loved ones who have passed away. There seems no rhyme or reason to the torments the nekomata might bring. It is for this reason that it is felt dangerous to keep a cat too long. But don't go killing it – or seven generations will be cursed.

Should you dispose of the cat or even just allow it to leave, it may end up a mountain nekomata. These are known to kill humans they come upon by chance, although many believe that a nekomata has the power to lure their prey to them by mimicking the cries of people who are in peril. In going up to save them, the new victim condemns themselves to a terrible death. Some say they can even assume human form, until they have the victim exactly where they want them.

Of course, it is highly unlikely if you own a cat that you will wake up to it trying to kill you, or that it will transform into a nekomata. But do keep an eye on any unusual animal behaviour, such as the cat appearing aloof or superior, suddenly digging its claws into you or making howling noises for no apparent reason. It may be that Kitty is ready for a transformation.

THE AUSTRALIAN HUGGER

In 1798, Captain John Hunter, the Governor of New South Wales in the new colony of Australia, sent back to England the pelt of a creature he had discovered, along with sketches of it. The best naturalists of the day dismissed it as a hoax. Someone had sewn a duck's bill onto an otter's body, they scoffed. The famous anatomist Robert Knox declared it the work of ingenious Asian taxidermists. It was a long time before experts agreed the platypus was a real animal.

Australia has long been home to creatures so exotic that they have beguiled Europeans – from porcupine-like beasts that lay eggs (echidnas), to deer-like beings that jump on their hind legs (kangaroos). It is thus no surprise that there are as many weird creatures yet to be classified as there are those that already have been. Perhaps the most terrifying of these is the Bunyip.

Anyone in Australia will tell you that it is only a matter of time before someone actually catches a Bunyip. These huge amphibious creatures reportedly inhabit the swamps and lagoons of the Australian interior and like nothing better than human prey, especially women and children. Accounts vary as to their appearance – they may resemble a hippopotamus, perhaps a sea cow or manatee. Others believe they have long necks and small heads. They may even have flippers.

They are also thought to be nocturnal and to produce a loud booming sound. This may be how the Bunyip protects the waterway it lives in – indigenous Australians will tell you that the quickest way to incur its wrath is to take more than your fair share of fish. Hence one should only take what one needs. This is why some regard the Bunyip as protectors of the environment – of which humans are just one part and not necessarily all that important.

Many European settlers also encountered Bunyips. The escaped convict William Buckley claimed to have seen them many times, although he said, "I could never see any part, except the back, which appeared to be covered with feathers of a dusky grey colour." The artist Edwin Stocqueler also encountered a Bunyip in the 1850s, describing it as "having two small fins attached to the shoulders, a long swan-like neck, a head like a dog and a curious bag hanging under the jaw, resembling the pouch of the pelican". He drew the creature but could not capture it, having only one bullet in his gun and a "very frail boat".

There were also many fossils found of quadrupeds much larger than buffaloes. One set of fossils was shown to a local indigenous group and they instantly told the explorer that they recognized it as a Bunyip, which their description made clear was a combination of bird and alligator, although with the head of an emu and legs like a frog's, which allowed it to swim at great speed. But when on shore it could walk erect and was known to be thirteen feet or more tall.

The sheer size of Australia has made finding the Bunyip very difficult, but still the search goes on. If you do encounter a Bunyip, bear one thing in mind. They say that its preferred method of killing is by hugging its victim, in the same way as a boa constrictor. Don't, whatever you do, mistake this for affection.

POPO BAWA

In Zanzibar in 1995, a series of attacks of the most dreadful kind took place. Men and women were assaulted in their beds and ravaged in unspeakable ways. In each case the victim originally thought they were dreaming as something pressed down on them. But this was no dream. It seems that this was the work of Popo Bawa, a Swahili name which translates as "bat wing". What made these attacks so terrible was not only their ferocity, but one outstanding feature: the Popo Bawa went after people who didn't believe in him.

The Popo Bawa is a hater of sceptics. Nothing enrages him more than those who deny his existence. He is believed to have originated on the island of Pemba, on the Zanzibar archipelago, and that was where in 1971 he took possession of a young girl and spoke in a deep voice through her. Only by believing in Popa Bawa would anyone be safe.

Since then, a number of Popa Bawa panics have spread across Zanzibar in waves – in 1970, 1995 and 2000, and then in Dar es Salaam in Tanzania in 2007. It was the one in 1995 that caught the world's attention, as mass hysteria broke out across the East African state. Whole villages would gather outside their homes at night, refusing to go to their beds lest Popo Bawa attacked. The government broadcast announcements appealing for calm.

But they had no effect. At least one visitor from Tanzania was killed by a mob in a frenzy when he was mistaken for Popo Bawa. Hopes that the creature had been vanquished were dashed the next night as the incidents continued.

They say he is a shape-shifter but generally takes the form of a large bat-like beast, hence his name. He is said to give off a foul odour, like sulphur burning. Some say his existence may have been triggered by the release of a djinn on the island of Pemba. Others say he has always existed but has become ever more furious at our loss of faith in the supernatural. Others yet say he is one of the shetani, evil spirits that have bedevilled East African nations for all of time. To keep them away you can hang a piece of paper from the ceiling inscribed with Islamic verses. Virtually all Zanzibarian houses and shops have one of these hanging. Allegedly, one can appease a shetani by sacrificing goats, cows or chickens and sprinkling their blood on all four corners of the room. But don't miss a day, or the shetani will demand a male child as a replacement.

But neither the hanging verses or the sacrifice of animals seem to have any effect on Papa Bowa. And if he is a shetani, all agree he is the worst.

For what could be worse than a creature whose main target is those who deny his existence? It is said that once Popo Bawa has finished his assault, he demands that the victim tell everyone they know what has happened, who it was that left them in this condition. Should they fail to do so, they can expect another visit, another violation in their bed.

A number of Western scholars have investigated the phenomenon of Popo Bawa panic, ascribing it to waking dreams, or mass hysteria, or confusion about what happens when old beliefs come into contact with new ones. Perhaps they are right, perhaps there is no such thing as Popo Bawa.

Only don't go telling him that.

WITCHCRAFT

"*Double, double, toil and trouble, fire burn and cauldron bubble, cool it down with baboon's blood, then the charm is fine and good.*"

As William Shakespeare will tell you, there is no one better at casting spells and seeing into the future than a witch. When his Weird Sisters saw that Macbeth would one day become king, they knew what they were talking about, but they also knew that it carried a curse that would be his downfall. If only he'd listened more carefully to that bit! But so spooky is this play that actors believe even saying its name brings on a curse. The Weird Sisters continue to work their magic...

Male or female, witches have haunted the imagination for the whole of human history. They are in the Bible, they are in Homer's Iliad *in the form of Circe. Most of all they are in the middle of the last millennium, when the witch craze spread across Europe and the United States.*

Even today they are feared and respected, and random outbreaks of hysteria occur, fingers are pointed, terrible prices are paid.

But however many times humanity thinks it has moved on, put the whole thing behind it, the witch comes back, performing magic for human good or evil, making potions, casting spells and telling us the future. Unlike Macbeth, we should always listen to the whole thing...

"*Adder's fork and blind-worm's sting, lizard's leg and howlet's wing, for a charm of powerful trouble, like a hell-broth, boil and bubble.*"

LA VOISIN

She was one of the best-connected women in seventeenth-century France, entertaining the Parisian aristocracy in the evenings with large garden parties and string quartet performances. Guests included noblemen and women, and even the official mistress of King Louis XIV.

During the day they were her clients, as Catherine Monvoisin, known as "La Voisin", was the greatest and wealthiest fortune-teller in all of France. Her services included selling aphrodisiacs (La Voisin was said to have had at least six lovers, so perhaps this worked) and other potions, palmistry and midwifery. And, it was said, performing abortions and dispensing poison. She also supplied amulets and performed sacred rituals.

These were said to include black masses, where she asked Satan to make her clients' wishes come true.

She was not the first woman accused in what became known as the Affair of the Poisons. That was Madame de Brinvilliers, who in 1675 was charged with the murder of her father. Brinvilliers was also alleged to have tested the poison on hospital patients, killing 30 of them. Found guilty, she was forced to drink 16 pints of water, before being beheaded and having her body burned at the stake. She was the first of 36 to be executed during the Affair, which saw 442 suspects and 218 arrests.

Two years later, the fortune-teller Magdelaine de La Grange was hanged for forgery and murder. In her confession she had revealed a network of fortune-tellers, alchemists and poisoners. The panicked king ordered arrests, and many were tortured into revealing the names of other poisoners. And the name mentioned most was La Voisin.

Arrested in 1679 and questioned while intoxicated, La Voisin admitted to organizing black masses and selling aphrodisiacs. There is no evidence she was tortured and some say this was because the king was nervous about who she would name if she was. All of Paris knew her connection to the aristocracy and to the king's court itself.

She denied ever meeting the king's mistress, saying only that "Paris is full of this kind of thing and there is an infinite number of people engaged in this evil trade." Reportedly, she chose not to divulge her connections lest the king be deposed.

After her arrest, a search was allegedly made of her garden and the bones of 2,500 babies found. No doubt this number was an exaggeration, but it is clear some of the children she had aborted for society women ended up here. But some say that at the black masses it was the blood of newborn babies which would be poured into the chalice. Did La Voisin offer to take away babies which had come to term and use them for her magic?

On 17 February 1680, La Voisin was put on trial for witchcraft. Two days later she was found guilty and sentenced to be burned at the stake. On 22 February she was led through the streets of Paris to the Place de Grève, where a hundred years later the guillotine would perform its deadly deeds. Thousands gathered to watch. It is said that when a priest came up to deliver the final sacrament she pushed him away.

We do not know her final words, but she may have cursed all who condemned her, including, finally, King Louis XIV himself. Did a witch's curse begin the French Revolution?

THE FIRST WITCHES

We don't know when the first witch appeared, but they likely existed in biblical times. The Book of Samuel, written between 930 and 721 BCE, makes the first ever mention of a witch – the Witch of Endor.

Allegedly, King Saul, who had driven all necromancers and magicians from Israel, called on the spirit of the prophet Samuel to tell him if his army would be victorious in battle against the Philistines. Receiving no answer, he sought a witch's counsel in the village of Endor.

Saul disguised himself and visited the witch at night. She refused to assist, due to his own edict against sorcery. Saul assured her she was safe and she summoned the spirit – an Elohim, the Hebrew word for a god, spirit or angel. The witch then realized who her visitor was and cried, "Why have you deceived me?"

Saul assured her again that she would not be punished and asked her to describe the Elohim, as the god was invisible to him. She told him he looked like an old man with a cloak. Saul bowed and the Elohim, through the witch, berated the king for disturbing him and disobeying God. He then gave Saul his prophecy – "The Lord will also deliver Israel with thee into the hand of the Philistines: and tomorrow shalt thou and thy sons be with me."

Saul collapsed and the Elohim departed. The witch fed him a calf to give him strength for the battle against the Philistines. But it did no good. As the Elohim had prophesied, Saul's army was defeated, his sons killed. Saul then fell on his own sword.

Some say this was part of Saul's punishment for consorting with witches and spirits rather than asking God. It may even have been that there was no Elohim, and that the witch worked her magic, not only to give the illusion that the spirit existed, but to cause Saul's downfall in combat. Who can know the power of witches?

It is hard to know how many witches there were in those ancient times. If Saul had to ban them, there may have been many, and the Book of Leviticus is full of warnings about "mediums" or those who "seek out spirits". Those who consult them will be "cut off from their people", while "A man or woman who is a medium or spiritist among you must be put to death. You are to stone them; their blood will be on their own heads."

If that wasn't enough, those who "practise the magic arts" will join murderers, the sexually immoral and the unbelieving in being cast onto a "fiery lake of burning sulphur". This, says the Lord, "will be a second death".

We also know that in the later New Testament the city of Ephesus was renowned for its sorcerers, and that as Christianity spread many sorcerers burned their books. "When they calculated the value of the scrolls, the total came to fifty thousand drachmas." Not cheap, then!

All we know is that witches have been with us for thousands of years, and that the advice from the holy has been the same since Moses led the slaves out of Egypt – "thou shalt not suffer a witch to live".

FOXY LADY

In Japan, witches are traditionally divided into two types, those whose sidekicks – called familiars – are snakes and those who are accompanied by foxes. The latter, called *kitsune-tsukai*, is more common.

They generally use the favourite foods of the fox to bring it into their lair and then persuade it to join its magical powers to theirs, making for an unbeatable combination! As in many cultures, the fox is seen as a kind of trickster and can shape-shift. They can even turn into women and trap men.

Woe betide you if you happen to encounter a fox who has paired up with a male kitsune-tsukai. They are the most evil of all and can even send their fox to take possession of other humans, to their absolute peril. Fortunately, these are rare, but one should never let one's guard down.

Nowadays the most common Japanese witches are called "magical girls" and are said to have been inspired by the Western television show *Bewitched*. They are much more benign; helpful, even. Unless this is some sort of smokescreen put up by a kitsune-tsukai...

ISOBEL GOWDIE

She first met the Devil in the dead of night outside a church at Auldearn in the Highlands of Scotland. To please him she renounced her baptism and allowed him to suck blood from her shoulder. He had, she said, cloven hooves. At other meetings they had sex, dug up a child's body from its grave in order to destroy the village's crops and performed rituals to inflict illness on the local minister. Together they made arrows which could kill victims at a distance, which no armour could withstand.

We don't know much about Isobel Gowdie, except that she was from the Auldearn area and was married to a man named John Gilbert. But what we do know is that her four confessions after her arrest for witchcraft in 1662 are the most detailed record we have of the activities of witches, not only in Scotland but all of Europe.

Gowdie was part of a coven, a group of witches that would gather at night and perform rituals and masses. During her confessions she said that she would place a broomstick beside her sleeping husband when she went out – some say this is why broomsticks and witches are associated with each other to this day.

According to Gowdie, the witches in the coven could transform themselves into animals. She gave her captors 27 chants which, when performed correctly, would trigger this transformation. She herself had been transformed into a cat and a jackdaw. The coven also made clay effigies of the children of the local lord, causing them to suffer and then die.

On another night, the coven was entertained by the Fairy Queen, who helped them fly through the air on horses and steal food from the houses of the rich. Another time she transformed into a hare but was chased by wild dogs and only narrowly escaped. While they would not have been able to kill her, any scars she suffered in hare form would have remained on her as a human.

Finally, she described the number of villagers she and the coven had killed, expressing regret for what she had done and divulging the names and nicknames of the other women in the coven. Whether she confessed under duress is not known, but torture was common during the Scottish witch trials of this time. Forty-one women were arrested based on her confession. If she thought candour would spare her, she was wrong – Gowdie was prosecuted for witchcraft and murder.

There is no record of her execution, but it is unlikely to have been any different to other witches in that area of that time. She likely would have been taken to Gallowhill on the outskirts of nearby Nairn, then strangled and burned. Her body would have been buried in unconsecrated ground, along with the other members of the coven. Having renounced baptism, perhaps they would have wished for no less.

Isobel Gowdie's confessions are still one of the most telling documents around for understanding what witches get up to in the middle of the night. She has become something of a folk hero, her story told in songs, books and plays. There has even been a symphony written about her. In Auldearn they still raise a glass to her, as they have not lived under a lord for hundreds of years – the male children of the last one died in very mysterious circumstances.

ARADIA

In 1899, the American folklorist Charles Godfrey Leland was in Italy when a fortune-teller from Tuscany named Maddalena handed him a book. She said it was a religious text belonging to a coven of Tuscan witches, who worshipped Aradia, the daughter of the Roman goddess Diana. The book contained what would become the basis of the twentieth-century religion of Wicca.

About Aradia herself we know very little. Some say she is in fact Herodias, the wife of King Herod, who asked for the head of John the Baptist on a plate and was condemned to wander the sky every night, only permitted to rest in the treetops from midnight to dawn. Is this how she came to join the nymphs of Diana, who supposedly make their nightly journey across the heavens? Or is she the daughter of the goddess? According to the book, Diana bore a child to the Sun, named Lucifer, who she later seduced while in the form of a cat, giving birth to Aradia. Diana sent Aradia to Earth as Queen of the Witches so she could teach the oppressed her magic and overthrow their tormentors.

The book itself, which Leland named *Arcadia, or the Gospel of the Witches*, includes his translation of Maddalena's own work, *Vangelo*, as well as chapters on rituals and magic spells. You can invoke Aradia to win love and good health, or to cause the opposite to your enemies. There is also an incantation to Laverna, the goddess of criminals, which shows that witches themselves are social disrupters, and a description of a witches' sabbath – a gathering of witches to carry out diabolical activities.

While some have questioned the book's authenticity – Maddalena later disappeared, perhaps in a puff of smoke – no one can doubt its influence. In the twentieth century it was taken up by Wiccans, who identified with its female-centred beliefs – the book claims that Diana created the world – and its embrace of magic.

Aradia's speech in the first chapter has become part of the Wiccan liturgy, with many believing that the nudity that is essential to Wicca is inspired by Aradia's words: "And as the sign that ye are truly free, ye shall be naked in your rites, both men and women." Others dispute this, saying that nudity has always been part of witchcraft; for instance, in Florence in 1375, a woman named Marta was tortured for allegedly having "placed candles round a dish and to have taken off her clothes and stood above the dish in the nude, making magical signs".

Wiccans also identify with Aradia's connection to nature, and some see her as the goddess of the whole world, sent by her mother the creator to look after nature in all its forms. To protect the world, one invokes Aradia, who will spread her magic over it and keep it from the evil ones.

No one knows how the rites of Italian witchcraft were passed down the ages – perhaps Diana herself was reponsible, or did Aradia oversee it? Had Charles Godfrey Leland not met a woman named Maddalena in Tuscany in 1899, perhaps the history of the world would be different. But the nightly train of Diana, Aradia and the nymphs across the sky will, they say, continue forever, spreading its magic.

HOW TO

Thinking of dabbling in witchcraft but not sure where to start? You could do a lot worse than picking up a copy of *Picatrix*, your handy how-to guide to all things witchy.

Originally written in Arabic in the tenth century, under the title *Ghāyat al-Ḥakīm*, which means roughly *The Aim of the Sage* or *The Goal of the Wise*, it has everything you need to know in getting started on your path to magical powers.

According to *Picatrix*, reality is made up of many different worlds or planes, and the way to make magic happen is to recognize this and get into the gaps between the worlds. From there you can bend reality to your will, including such things as changing your form, commanding animals and smiting your enemies.

Some have noted its correspondence with Jewish kabbalism, and some with Islamic religious thought, and it definitely resonates with Christian and even Hindu thoughts about reality. Something for everybody! But you don't have to be a believer to get involved. *Picatrix* has been a source book for everyone from atheists to Satanists.

But be careful in there. Once you've read it, your view of reality might be changed forever!

MOTHER SHIPTON

Every parent has had that scary experience. They have turned their back for just a moment and lost their child, at least briefly. In 1490, the poor mother of Ursula Sontheil popped out to run a few errands in the small town of Knaresborough in North Yorkshire, England. We can imagine how anxious she was when she returned to find the door open and her two-year-old gone.

The child had already proved unusual, to say the least. They say she was born ugly and deformed, with a hunchback and bulging eyes, during a terrible thunderstorm. Instead of crying the baby cackled and the storm instantly stopped.

Ursula's mother gathered her neighbours to search for the child. They heard a wail "like a thousand cats" and looked everywhere. They found Ursula perched on the iron rail above the fireplace, naked and cackling.

This is the first of the legends of Mother Shipton, the famous witch of North Yorkshire, who baby Ursula would grow up to be. Others soon grew around her. So frightened were the villagers of this demonic child that she and her mother were exiled to a cave. Locals believed she was Satan's spawn and the skull-shaped pool in the cave attested to her evil.

As Ursula grew, her hunchback remained, as did her bulging eyes. Her nose and legs were crooked. The depiction of witches we are used to from old children's books are thought to be based on Mother Shipton's unfortunate physical disadvantages from back when physical deformities were equated with evil.

Alone in her cave, she taught herself the secrets of plants and herbs, their magic and healing properties. Although the townsfolk still reviled her, they soon appreciated her abilities as a herbalist. She also began to display supernatural powers – a woman whose coat had been stolen approached Ursula and asked her to divine who took it. She told her immediately, and the coat was recovered.

Soon after, she met a carpenter, Tobias Shipton, and was married, taking the name Mother Shipton. The townsfolk thought she had bewitched him, their suspicions only growing when he died two years later. Once again she was chased out of town; once again she dwelt in her cave.

But her spells remained popular, as did her ability to tell fortunes. More and more people came to consult Mother Shipton, and her prophecies became bolder and bolder. She began to prophesize about world events, and like her contemporary Nostradamus in France, her words became world famous. Even King Henry VIII spoke of the "Witch of York"; some believe she predicted the shortness of his marriages and his break with the Church.

She is also said to have predicted the defeat of the Spanish Armada in 1588 and the Great Fire of London in 1666 – the great diarist Samuel Pepys records his friends and family at the time discussing the fire and Mother Shipton's prediction.

In 1561, at the age of 73, Mother Shipton died, and the townsfolk who had driven her out twice now celebrated her as Knaresborough's heroine. The adulation continues to this day, with a number of pubs in the area named Mother Shipton. And in 2013, the townsfolk raised £35,000 to erect a statue of her.

And the cave? It is now England's oldest tourist attraction, having been open to the public since 1630. Many still go there to seek a cure for what ails them. For all her powers, one doubts the "Witch of York" could have predicted that!

THE SALEM WITCH TRIALS

In February 1692, in a Massachusetts village, the nine-year-old daughter of Reverend Samuel Parris, Betty Parris, and her cousin, 11-year-old Abigail Williams, began to have fits. They screamed, threw things about the room and contorted themselves into strange shapes. They said they could feel pins being stuck into them. Doctors found nothing wrong. Soon other young children began suffering the same pains and having the same fits. To local preachers the cause was obvious – this was witchcraft, and the perpetrators needed to be arrested. Samuel Parris asked the girls, "Who torments you?" They named three townsfolk: Tituba, Sarah Osborne and Sarah Good. The Salem Witch Trials had begun.

The first arrested was Tituba, the Bajan (Barbadian) slave of Samuel Parris, who cared for the children. At first she denied everything, but after being beaten she admitted she had given the girls "witch cake". She also claimed to have conversed with the Devil about hurting the kids.

Sarah Good was from a well-to-do family, but since her father's death she had been reduced to begging. Parris had taken her in for a while, but he kicked her out because she was "so turbulent a spirit, spiteful and so maliciously bent". Allegedly, when she appeared in court the children moaned and rocked back and forth, such was her power.

Sarah Osborne had been married to Robert Prince and had two sons. When he died she had remarried and declared that her widow's estate belonged to her and her new husband, rather than her sons, as Robert Prince had wished. Osborne was seen as overturning social norms. Moreover, her legal battles had left her stricken with depression. She was, to some, a mad woman.

From then on, the trials spiralled out of control. Anyone accused of witchcraft would accuse others. Between February 1692 and May 1693, 200 were brought to trial in a town with a population of only 500. Over 150 of them were women. Sarah Good's daughter was only four when accused. The accusers were young too. One, 17-year-old Elizabeth Hubbard, had 17 people arrested and 13 hanged by her testimony.

Once the "witch" was arrested, various methods were employed to build the "case". There were beatings and tortures. There was also the "touch test" – the accused was brought into the presence of someone having a fit; if they touched them and the fit stopped, this was evidence of dark magic.

Finally, the Salem courts admitted "spectral evidence". If the victim could see the apparition of the person afflicting them, they could report it. Some felt this was controversial – couldn't the Devil take on any shape to persecute his prey? After a long debate the court agreed the Devil could only take on a person's shape with their permission. Thus a victim seeing an apparition meant not only was the person a witch but that they had communicated with the Devil.

In May 1693 the trials halted suddenly. Of the three first accused, Tituba, who had been imprisoned for 13 months, was re-sold and never heard of again. Sarah Osborne never came to trial and died in prison. Sarah Good was hanged, crying to the judge as she was led to the gallows, "I'm no more a witch than you are a wizard, and if you take away my life God will give you blood to drink." Legend has it that the judge later died by choking on his own blood...

WITCH-SPOTTING

It can be hard to identify witches. By their nature they are tricksy and they often dwell among normal humans without drawing attention to themselves.

Those prosecuting at the Salem Witch Trials used various methods. You could weigh a witch against a stack of Bibles. If the accused was heavier or lighter than them, they were deemed a witch. Only if the scales were level were they innocent. One of the first accused, Sarah Good, was convicted for talking to herself – which apparently meant she was casting spells.

Witches were also alleged to be unable to recite the Lord's Prayer. The parson George Burroughs was almost freed when he was able to recite the prayer while standing on the gallows. But in a catch-22, the judge argued that this was simply more evidence of his sorcery – Burroughs must have allowed the Devil to speak through him. He was hanged.

In 1710, Dorko Boda from Hungary was forced to undertake the "swimming test". Witches are not baptized, so when you throw them in a lake, the lake will reject them and they will float. If the accused sinks, they are innocent and ought to be rescued, but if they float they are definitely a witch. Poor old Dorko floated and so was burned at the stake.

It is also common knowledge that a witch's familiars – the cats, bats and rats who accompany them – need to be suckled every 24 hours. Keep the familiars away from the witch and all other foods, and they will die. Alternatively, drill a hole in the wall of the witch's house and watch for any suckling.

But make no assumptions about the type of familiar. In 1645, the witch John Bysack admitted that he had six snails as his familiars. Twenty years earlier he had been visited by the Devil in the form of a dog, who told Bysack to renounce God, Christ and his baptism. He did so, and the Devil used his claw to scratch Bysack's heart as part of the oath. The six snails then fed on his blood. They all had names, and they would kill particular animals on Bysack's orders. Atleward killed cows, Jeffry killed pigs, Peter killed sheep, Pyman killed fowls and Sacar killed horses. Most terrifying of all was Sydrake. He killed Christians.

At around the same time, Margaret Wyard confessed to having seven familiars, including flies and mice. It was noted, however, that she only had five breasts, so her truthfulness was called into question. Lying about being a witch was also punishable by death, and so she died at the stake.

But perhaps the most reliable way to identify a witch is to ask the victim of the possession who it is doing them harm. This need not stop when the victim dies. In the olden days in Ghana there was the practice of corpse-carrying. If someone had been killed by a witch, the villagers would carry the body around from house to house, and the corpse would point at the killer. The guilty party could then either be killed or sold into slavery, thus ridding the village of the evil-doer – although it seems another one would always arrive soon after.

SKINWALKERS

Skinwalkers. The name is creepy enough, even before they get around to working their evil on you. A skinwalker is a Navajo witch, whose trick is to take possession of animals or humans and walk around in them, hence the name. Unlike medicine men, who are good witches, skinwalkers are anything but.

One is not born a skinwalker; you need to go through a magical initiation, which means performing the evilest deed a mortal can do, which generally means murder, preferably of a sibling. If you are willing to be so evil as a mortal, imagine the evil you can do once transformed! This is why it is forbidden in Navajo culture to wear the pelts of predators – it's a slippery slope.

Once you become a skinwalker, you can then adopt the skin of anything you want, but the nice thing is you're not stuck with it. Some of them wear animal skulls or antlers atop their heads, bringing them more power.

The difficulty of catching a skinwalker – if one ever wanted to – is that they can keep transforming themselves, especially when pursued. They are said to run faster than a car and have the ability to jump high cliffs.

The evil society of the witches gathers in dark caves or secluded places to carry out their evil tasks – to initiate new members, harm people from a distance with black magic and perform dark ceremonial rites. They are also quite happy to read others' minds, controlling their thoughts and behaviour, causing disease and illness and even death.

If this wasn't enough, it is believed that skinwalkers can control the creatures of the night – such as owls and wolves – and make them do their bidding. They can even reanimate the corpses of the dead and make them carry out terrible tasks or commit murder. One should not go out at night if there is any sense of a skinwalker being about – which there always is.

It is not just the Navajo who live in the southwestern states who encounter them, of course. There is one story of a farmer hearing laughter coming from his sheep pens. He went to investigate and saw all of the sheep but one huddled in a corner shaking. He saw the missing one on the other side of the room, standing on its hind legs and laughing. The farmer must have been lucky that day; the laughing sheep then went back on all fours and rejoined the flock.

So keep an eye out for skinwalkers. They say you can kill them by shooting them in the head with bullets dipped in white ash. But don't miss – there is nothing scarier than a skinwalker out for revenge!

THE MARRIAGE BREAKER

There are witches and there are vampires. Both are scary, but each demands a different approach if we mortals are to stay reasonably safe – apologies to any immortals who may be reading this.

But what about – a vampire-witch? Unfortunately for those of us who like a quiet life, these terrible hybrids are not unheard of. Some say they are the offspring of a vampire and a witch; some say they are witches who happen to have been bitten by a vampire. It probably doesn't matter too much if you find yourself confronted with one – unless you use it as a conversation starter.

What is known is that your average vampire-witch is able to combine the skills of a vampire – superhuman abilities (strength, speed, stamina, agility, reflexes and durability), immortality, the ability to fly, to shapeshift, hypnotize and heal – with the skills of a witch – the capacity for magic, warping reality, necromancy, mind control, spell-casting and clairvoyance. You do not want to get on their bad side.

Of course, in real life, a vampire-witch may be more limited in what it can do. Perhaps the most famous vampire-witches, called chedipes, are said to haunt the area around the Godavari River in India, and few who encounter them live to tell the tale.

Some say that chedipes are the undead offspring of women who have died an unnatural death, such as in childbirth or by suicide. They are often seen either riding a tiger or assuming the form of one. But you can tell it is a chedipe, as one leg retains its human form. This is known as Murulupuli, the Enchanting Tiger, as many a man has been seduced by this one shapely leg.

She reputedly brings impurity into a happy home, by breaking the marriage bond between husband and wife. She will make love to the man while his wife sleeps, or leave her scent in his bed during the day to arouse suspicion. Many a man has been a victim of this. The chedipe enjoys sadness and pain that comes from the betrayal of a spouse.

But, being a vampire, a chedipe also loves blood. In accord with her erotic nature, she does not extract the blood of her victims as per normal vampires. Instead, she targets the toes. She will enter the marriage bed of a man and suck each toe to take his blood. However pleasurable it may feel at the time, in the morning he remembers nothing. But he feels weaker and his skin is paler. Night after night the chedipe does this, and the man loses his ability to satisfy his wife. It is said that a man in this condition should check his toes for bite marks and either consult a doctor or employ an exorcist. If he is not treated, he will wither and die.

The chedipe has also been known to pluck out the tongue of her victim, so he can no longer tell his wife that he loves her. Many a man has died from this in shame. So she takes her revenge on human happiness.

There are many vampire-witches and some say that a chedipe is the least destructive. But if you are a man and you find yourself fatigued and unable to fulfil your conjugal duties, beware. You might have been visited, and worse is to come...

THE PAPPENHEIMERS

We know from Shakespeare that witches often come in threes. But what happens when there is a whole family of witches? And what if their punishment far exceeds the most malignant activities of the witches themselves?

In 1600, Germany, like the rest of Europe was swept up in the witch craze. While the conventional punishments were deemed sufficient elsewhere, Bavarians felt that only extreme methods of torture would act as a deterrent against those tempted into sorcery and other such nefarious activities.

So it was that the Pappenheimer family got caught up in a hideous case of judicial violence.

Paulus and Anna and their three sons, Gummprecht, Michel and Hansel were vagrants. They supported themselves by going around the country emptying cess pits and digging graves – the lowest-status jobs available.

A thief, arrested by the Bavarian authorities, accused two of the Pappenheimers' sons of being his accomplices in killing several pregnant women. Before he was executed, he said that while he had only murdered for money, the Pappenheimers wanted the dead babies. They were, he swore, for ungodly purposes.

The Pappenheimers were hunted down, arrested and jailed.

At first the third and youngest, Hansel, was left with their landlord, but not knowing what to do with the boy, the landlord soon turned him in to the authorities.

Bavaria at the time was lawless, with many unsolved crimes. Its duke saw an opportunity both to make the treatment of the Pappenheimers an incentive to not misbehave and to "solve" some unsolved cases.

Hansel was tortured first, as it was felt that as a child he would break first. He did, but none of the crimes he confessed to existed. So the adults were tortured next. They were beaten, burned by torches and underwent a *strappado* (the victim is hung on a rope with their hands behind their back for hours, causing dislocated shoulders and then death).

In the end they confessed to every unsolved crime in Bavaria. They also named 400 accomplices, many of whom did not exist. As well as the crimes of this Earth, they confessed that they had made a pact with the Devil, promising to get him the hands of children for his spells, in return for money and possessions. This is why they had killed the pregnant women.

In the end all of the Pappenheimers were found guilty: Paulus for slaying 100 children, robbing ten churches, violently slaying 44 adults and setting fire to eight barns; Anna for also slaughtering 100 children, dispatching 19 old people with spells, burning barns and poisoning meadows to kill cows "so often that she herself cannot tell the number"; Gummprecht for killing 30 children and 24 adults, and torching nine homes and "causing strife between God-fearing spouses on four occasions"; and Michel for murdering 65 infants, setting five fires and causing ten gales and hailstorms.

If the torture was horrible, the executions were worse. First they were injured with hot tongs before having their arms broken on a wheel. Paulus was impaled on a stake. Then the whole family were burned alive.

Through all of this Hansel was forced to watch to deter him from future witchcraft. Soon afterwards he was rebaptized as Cyprian and welcomed into the Church.

But the duke was having none of it. Three weeks later they killed Hansel too.

WARLOCKS

"Warlock" – the name just doesn't quite inspire the same fear as "witch". It sounds more like a mighty lord of some sort, or a wise seer from *The Lord of the Rings*. Anyone can be a witch, male or female, and more often than not these days "witch" is being used across genders.

In fact, the word "warlock" originally meant "a breaker of oaths" or "a deceiver", and it was only in Scotland that it meant something like a witch. In making a pact with the Devil, a warlock was felt to have broken his oath with God.

One chap happy to be called a warlock was Abramelin the Mage, whose fifteenth-century *Book of Sacred Magic* raced off the shelves in his day. As well as practical advice on warlocking, casting spells and so on, it is best known for introducing "magic word squares". Each square casts a magical spell, and each row makes sense on its own, and contributes to the spell. A sort of fifteenth-century Sudoku, but the pay-off at the end, where your enemy is smote, or your pigeon turns into a bat, is much, much better.

THE LOUDON POSSESSION

Loudon is thought to be one of the prettiest towns in France, and residents would be happy if it was best known for its antique monuments, winding old streets and Roman archaeological site. In fact, it's more (in)famous for one of the most remarkable incidents in the history of witchcraft.

It was 1632. An outbreak of the plague had torn through the town, and most of the residents were either dead or locked away in their houses. In addition, a dispute had broken out about whether to demolish the city walls. The town was divided. There was a climate of fear and suspicion.

Enter a new parish priest, the handsome and eloquent Urbain Grandier. Popular in the town, he incurred the jealousy of a number of the monks at the local monastery. Also jealous were many of the town's husbands, as Grandier was a little overfamiliar with the female population. He was rumoured to have fathered a child with at least one. One aggrieved party attacked him in the street. Briefly banned from performing his priestly duties, he resumed once acquitted.

In Loudon there was a convent of 17 nuns. Shortly after the plague outbreak, some of the nuns started seeing visions. A demon of lust, Asmodai, was making them perform nefarious activities.

The nuns' behaviour grew more erratic. They shouted, swore and barked like dogs. Crowds gathered outside the convent to watch the bizarre spectacle. Eventually the Archbishop of Bordeaux intervened and locked the nuns away. They were also questioned as to who was causing the magic. All gave the same answer – Urbain Grandier.

Grandier was arrested and placed in Angers jail. The nuns were dispersed into other convents. Each in turn was brought before a bishop, who attempted to exorcise them. He failed to do so. It was instead decided that Grandier himself should perform the exorcisms. He succeeded in each case, but every success made it more likely that he was the sorcerer, so the authorities believed. Thus, he was sentenced to be burned at the stake.

They say that he begged for clemency, and that this was rejected. He asked to say a few final words before he died and this was granted. He was also told that he would be hanged before being burned, the usual act of mercy. This did not happen.

Taken to the pyre, he began to speak to the crowd, but the angry mob – perhaps a jealous husband or two – threw water in his face and drowned out his words. The fire was lit. As the executioner approached to strangle him, the flames shot up, burning the rope and claiming the "witch of Loudon". His screams could be heard, they say, all the way to the distant convent.

But if the authorities thought that was the end of it, they were wrong. The possessions continued for some three years after his death. The Mother Superior, Jeanne des Anges, woke one morning to find the names Joseph and Mary inscribed on her skin. Later, a vision appeared and informed her that she and all the nuns would be freed if she made a pilgrimage to the tomb of St Francis des Sales, author of the Treatise on the Love of God.

This she did. And the Loudon Possession ended.

THE WITCHES OF WARBOYS

The Fens in England have always been creepy. Reclaimed land, it is marshy and windswept. Many ghost stories have been set in the Fens, but perhaps the most terrifying tale is that of the Witches of Warboys.

Jane Throckmorton, the daughter of the rich village squire, was only nine when it happened. She started having fits followed by uncontrollable sneezing, for hours at a time. Her belly swelled so much she could not bend double and then she would get the shakes. Her older sisters were petrified – "Take her away, look where she standeth here before us in a black thrumbed cap. It is she that hath bewitched us and she will kill us if you do not take her away!" But soon they too fell ill, the eldest daughter, Joan, worst of all.

Soon the servants were also suffering fits. These too could last hours, and after recovering they remembered nothing. And when a servant was replaced, the new one got it just as bad. The Throckmortons began to suspect that there was no rational explanation. It had to be witchcraft.

Suspicion fell on the Throckmortons' 76-year-old neighbour, Alice Samuel. Like other neighbours she visited the girls to enquire after their health; unlike other neighbours, the girls were terrified by her. "Did you ever see one more like a witch than she is?" they said. They thought she was responsible for their suffering.

Soon the whole village was swept up in the panic – there were rumours that Alice Samuel, her daughter Agnes and husband John visited the graveyard at night, and that the old woman made potions of an unearthly nature. Was she envious of the five privileged girls? Did she bewitch them as revenge for her own poverty?

Their father, Robert Throckmorton, was a friend of Sir Henry Cromwell, whose grandson would be Oliver Cromwell, who led the English Revolution. Sir Henry's wife, Lady Cromwell, paid a visit to Alice Samuel after hearing the accusations the girls made. The moment she met Alice, Lady Cromwell was also convinced she was a witch. Grabbing a pair of scissors, she cut out a lock of Alice Samuel's hair, which she gave to Mrs Throckmorton to burn, believing this to be a remedy for witchcraft. But if Lady Cromwell thought she had beaten the witch, she was wrong.

That night, Lady Cromwell had a nightmare. And the night after that and the night after that. It was well known that witches can enter one's dreams and manipulate them – had Alice Samuel cursed Lady Cromwell? Again the village was in uproar, which only grew worse shortly after – when Lady Cromwell dropped dead. She had died childless, and the graves of both her and her widowed husband would be destroyed in the Civil War started by their grandson.

The death of Lady Cromwell confirmed what everyone had long believed. Alice Samuel was a witch. She was put on trial, as were her husband and daughter. All were found guilty of bewitching the Throckmorton children, and for the death of Lady Cromwell. They were taken and hanged. Some say that when the jailer examined Alice Samuel's corpse he found on it a witch's mark, a symbol used to indicate that people believed her to be a witch.

The girls recovered the moment Alice Samuel was hanged and were never ill again. Strangely, their mother died almost immediately after Alice Samuel – and their father, the squire, mysteriously left town, never to be heard of again...

FOOLED YOU!

A quick word of warning: it's possible to look for magic where there isn't any, and for clever people to manipulate the credulous.

The sixteenth-century mathematician John Napier had something of a reputation as a witch, given the amount of time he spent in his study playing with numbers. Also, he had invented a machine for multiplying numbers as large as four digits, which was called "Napier's Bones"; it was, after all, invented by Napier, and was made of bones. He also came up with ways of attacking ships at sea from the land in the catchily titled essay "Secret inventions, profitable and necessary in these days for defence of this island". A witch indeed.

Napier knew of his reputation and decided to put it to good use. It had become clear that one of his staff was stealing from him, so he gathered them all together and told them that in the totally dark room next door was a black rooster. They all had to go in and stroke the rooster. The one who made the rooster crow was the thief.

In they all trooped. A little while later, the rooster crowed. The thief was found and confessed.

What they hadn't realised is that Napier had covered the rooster in black soot, and that the thief would be too scared to stroke it, and so would come out with clean hands!

BABA YAGA

Somewhere, deep in the Slavic forest – the Russians say it is in Russia, the Romanians Romania, the Bulgarians Bulgaria – there is the most astonishing cottage in the world.

From a distance it looks perfectly normal – a roof, windows, chimney. But as you get closer, you'll notice the fence made of human skulls and a gate using the bones of human feet as hinges.

Then you'll see a house that appears to be hovering above the undergrowth. At the clearing you will see that the house stands on four chicken legs and will turn to face you as you approach. The smell is overwhelming.

This is the house of Baba Yaga, the scariest witch in Europe.

When she is at home, she rests on the stove and is so big that her nose touches the ceiling. As is unfortunately so often the case with legends of this nature, disfigurement is used as a shorthand for evil in descriptions of her – so her face is described as hideous and deformed, her legs bony, and some say she has iron teeth which help her to eat her favourite meal – children.

Above the house, a flock of black geese circles at her command. When she grows hungry, she can send one of the geese to snatch a child in its beak to bring to her cooking pot.

Parents warn their children to never go out when geese are flying. If they see a black goose, they should run home. Few make it back – a goose can fly faster than a child can sprint.

Or they might see Baba Yaga herself. She might be flying on a mortar with a pestle to steer her. Or she might be riding a pig as ugly as she. Don't be fooled by the pig – it can also outrun a child.

Reportedly, she is the creation of the Devil and the first of all witches. It is said that the Devil wanted to capture the essence of evil, so he cooked 12 nasty women together in a cauldron. As they cooked, he gathered the steam in his mouth, rolling it around to add his own evil saliva. Then he spat in the pot and out came Baba Yaga, more horrifying than even the Devil could have imagined.

So taken is the Devil with his evil creation, he will sometimes let her accompany him as he searches the world for the newly dead – he can have their souls and she can have their bodies for her pot.

Allegedly, she can transform into other creatures, and she has even been said to do good when taking the form of a princess or a common woman. Or perhaps she just uses these other forms to win the trust of children she will later devour?

All that is known is that Slavic mothers and fathers warn their children not to go out at night, or to be disobedient – Baba Yaga has a particular fondness for the taste of bad children and she can smell them from a mile away. Good children taste much blander, so the best thing a kid can do is behave well and do what Mummy and Daddy tell them.

And keep an eye on the sky for black geese.

PICK A CARD, ANY CARD

It was the French poet and occultist Éliphas Lévi who is credited with bringing together Tarot cards and witchcraft, as if each weren't powerful enough by themselves. Lévi, born Alphonse Louis Constant, was a prolific esoteric author. Many of the symbols we associate with twentieth-century black magic and witchcraft are based on his ideas – like pentagrams and Baphomet, the goat-like deity allegedly worshipped by the Knights Templar. Lévi purportedly coined the word "occultism" as a catch-all for supernatural activities.

Tarot cards have of course been around for a lot longer, originating in fourteenth-century Germany. They were popular in Italy a century after that, with the invention of printing boosting sales later. Before printing they had been hand-painted and only available to the very rich – perhaps some of their alleged mystical power came from this.

While it was the eighteenth-century magician Etteilla who started to use Tarot for occult purposes, it was Lévi's blending of the cards with esoterica that influenced future magi like the notorious Aleister Crowley. Tarot, they say, can help divine the future – and alter it.

Unlike Crowley, Lévi tended to use his supernatural skills for good rather than evil. The son of a shoemaker, he remained humble about his powers. He called himself "A poor and obscure scholar [who] has found the lever of Archimedes, and he offers it to you for the good of humanity alone, asking nothing whatsoever in exchange."

He also warned anyone wanting to follow his ways: "Let those, therefore, who seek in magic the means to satisfy their passions, pause in that deadly path, where they will find nothing but death or madness. This is the significance of the vulgar tradition that the Devil finished sooner or later by strangling the sorcerers."

PLAY TIME!

Robert the Doll sits, 40 inches tall, in a glass case in the Fort East Martello Museum in Key West, Florida. He still wears the white sailor suit his owner, the long-deceased painter Robert Eugene Otto, dressed him in when he was a child.

Robert is disturbing to look at. His face is worn away, covered in nicks and scratches. His eyes are black and beady. He himself has his own toy, a crazy-looking dog on his lap. On Robert's face is a permanent – and chilling – smirk, like he's just thought of an evil trick to play. His story is shrouded in witchcraft.

They say that Robert was given to Otto by a girl from the Bahamas, by way of apology for something bad she had done to him. It is also said that as a young boy, Otto experimented with voodoo, West African black magic.

More likely is that the doll was given to Otto by his grandfather for his birthday in 1904. Whichever back story is true, Otto and Robert became inseparable. While Otto was a very well-behaved boy, Robert was known to make messes and break things out of sheer mischief. Some think that it was by blaming Robert for every mishap that Otto unleashed the doll's occult abilities.

Because small breakages were only the beginning. People passing the house when Otto was a child, and even when he was an adult, would see Robert standing in the window, even when Otto was out, and allegedly see Robert at a different window before his owner got back. Visitors to the house reported sounds of footsteps and giggling from upstairs. Moreover, there were many fatal car crashes in the quiet street beside the house.

When Otto died, the new homeowner, Myrtle Reuter, took possession of the doll. She got used to him moving around the house and would come home to find he had shifted since she had been out. She swore that Robert's expression would grow angry if anything negative was said about Otto.

One journalist who visited said that on seeing Robert, "It was like a metal bar running down my back. At first when we walked through the door, the look on his face was like a little boy being punished. It was as if he was asking himself, 'Who are these people in my room and what are they going to do to me?'"

Robert was donated to the museum, where he now sits impassively in his glass case. But he doesn't seem to have stopped his activities. Electrical devices often fail around him and the cleaners at night swear they sometimes hear footsteps in his room.

Most troubling, the museum is inundated with letters and emails from recent visitors, asking staff to apologize for not treating Robert with enough respect. The hope is that this will lift the hex which the visitors claim has been placed on them since they encountered the doll.

While there is no proof that the car accidents or the difficulties visitors experience are down to Robert, and while he has never been witnessed doing any actual harm, the museum keeps the glass case firmly locked, apart from once a year when he is taken out and cleaned. This is always done by more than one staff member – being alone with Robert is too risky. As one person put it, "There is some kind of intelligence there. The doll is listening to us."

BLOCKULA

They say the Devil stays in a large house built on a large field that has no visible end. To get there, you have to go on a magical flight. Witches tended to fly there on broomsticks, fence posts or on the backs of sleeping men. Some would be clutching a child they had brought as a gift for the Devil. This is the island of Blockula, and it has been part of Swedish folklore for centuries.

The Devil received the witches in an immense hall, dressed in "a grey Coat, and red and blue Stockings: He had a red Beard, a high-crown'd Hat, with Linnen of divers Colors, wrapt about it, and long Garters upon his Stockings." Each witch would then cut their finger to sign the Devil's book in blood and pledge allegiance to him.

Those witches the Devil favoured sat closest to him during the following feast and knew they would be sharing his bed that night.

The feast would carry on deep into the night. There was dancing, fighting and cursing. Then the Devil would produce a harp and play his devilish music, before selecting the women he liked best to join him in his bedchamber. There he would ravish them and if he felt like it, carry out beatings until they were "black and blue". Some of the women became pregnant, and the Devil, rather gruesomely, would take their sons and daughters and marry them to each other.

When the children had their own babies, they took the shape of toads and serpents, and to this day all such creatures are thought by some to be the spawn of the Devil. Some witches also told of a great dragon on a chain, which the Devil threatened to release and cause havoc in all the land if they were not obedient.

It was to one of these gatherings that Märet Jonsdotter, the first woman executed for being a witch in Sweden, is said to have taken the 12-year-old Gertrud Svendsdotter. The girl had been seen walking on water and confessed that she had been to Blockula many times since she was eight. Märet Jonsdotter had taken her there; they had dined with Satan and smeared themselves in red oil. It was this oil on her feet that allowed her to walk on water.

She also took other children there, where their names were written in a book with black pages, as they were now the Devil's property. She described the mad feasts, where "Satan sat under the table and laughed so that the whole room shook and the fire of hell poured up from a hole in the floor, where you could see the tormented souls in hell." Everything there was done backwards – people danced with their backs to each other. People married multiple partners at once and women gave birth to frogs, which were then turned into butter.

Soon after, Märet Jonsdotter's young siblings were questioned and confessed they too had been to Blockula. They too had written their names in blood and had sex with the Devil. It was their older sister who had taken them, she was the Devil's favourite.

Throughout Märet refused to confess, even when the priest

told her that confession would mean she went to heaven after death. A Devil's mark was found on her finger, which sealed her guilt and she was burned at the stake.

The island of Blockula has never been found.

THE WITCH GHOST
OF RHODE ISLAND

Sometimes it's not enough just to be a witch. For one woman, her death by hanging in 1849 was only part one of her horrible legacy. She then became a ghost. With a name like Bathsheba Sherman, what else could she do?

We don't know much about the early life of Bathsheba Sherman, but we do know that she was seen as quite a catch when she married a prosperous farmer with 200 acres in Rhode Island. Did the local women regard her beauty as a threat?

The first sign of trouble came when she was babysitting a neighbour's son. The neighbour came home to find the child dead. A doctor's examination showed that the boy's skull had been impaled by a sharp spike. Like a knitting needle.

Bathsheba was never charged.

Soon after Bathsheba herself became pregnant and gave birth to a beautiful baby boy. Legend has it that a week later, her husband came home to find his wife stabbing the new baby. As he tried to grab her, Bathsheba hissed at him and declared her allegiance to the Devil. Flinging the baby in the fire, she then ran into the garden, climbed a tree and hanged herself. To the locals she was a witch, and the children had died in a blood sacrifice.

Time passed. Over a hundred years. When the Perrons – truckdriver Roger, his wife Carolyn and their five daughters – moved into the house in 1970, they knew nothing of the story of Bathsheba. They would get to know her very soon.

At first it was simply things going missing, noises coming from empty rooms, screams in the night. But then the girls started getting... visitors. A boy who gave his name as Oliver Richardson told the sisters that he was sad because he was trapped in the house.

Roger and Carolyn were sceptical until the ghosts started visiting them too. Dirt would materialize in rooms where no one had been. The noises increased. One of the daughters, Andrea, was visited by what she found to be an evil female spirit. Although the woman was beautiful she had a bent neck – like someone who had been hanged. Andrea was convinced this spirit wished to be the mistress of the house.

A local historian told them the story of Bathsheba Sherman. In fact, the farm had been in Sherman hands for centuries and it turned out there had been many enigmatic deaths. Perhaps the house itself had driven Bathsheba Sherman mad?

The Perron family sought out professional help and held a séance in the house. According to the family, the moment they started, Carolyn Perron's body contorted into a ball. The girls watched their mother in horror as she was then thrown against the floors and the walls. The chair she was sitting on levitated and her screams were deathly.

And then... she was alright. Whoever or whatever had possessed Carolyn Perron left and was never seen or felt again. A few years later an investigation of the local graveyard uncovered the memorial stone of Bathsheba Sherman. The woman who legend said had hung herself in 1849 died, according to the gravestone, in 1885 after a long, happy life. Had the legends been lies? Or had the possession of Carolyn Perron changed time itself and allowed the soul of Bathsheba Sherman to live a different, better life?

THE EXORCISM OF ANNE ECKLUND

She is known as Anne Ecklund, although nobody is sure if that was really her name – several other possibilities are given. We do know she was born in 1882 in Wisconsin, that her mother died when she was young and was a devout Catholic in her youth.

Her father, Jakob, was no such thing. Often drunk, he mocked the Church and its ministers. He allegedly had an affair with Mina, who was either his sister or stepsister. Mina had a reputation for performing black magic and was openly called a witch in the street. It is thought that Jakob also suggested that his daughter enter into an incestuous relationship with him.

It was around the age of 14 that Anna's behaviour changed. She started to find religious images repulsive, and said there was an invisible barrier which prevented her from entering churches. Her language grew foul and sexual and she was accused of taking part in "unspeakable sexual acts".

She was diagnosed as being possessed, and many believed it was her aunt Mina who had done this to her. Church authorities were called in, and an exorcism performed by

Father Theophilus Riesinger. Little is known about this exorcism, except that it seemed to work, and Anna returned to the Church.

After her father died, however, Anna resumed her strange behaviour. Religious items repulsed her, and she claimed to hear voices in her head. She was suddenly able to speak different languages and foamed at the mouth. She was again diagnosed as possessed, and Father Riesinger was brought in.

Anna was taken to a convent in Earling, Iowa. What happened there would be published in a 1935 pamphlet called *Begone Satan!*, which would cause such a stir that Riesinger would end up on the cover of *Time* magazine.

The nuns took turns guarding Anna between sessions. Despite not being able to eat, she vomited 20 or 30 times a day. Between times she was either comatose, speaking in different languages or making bestial sounds.

Riesinger ascertained there were five demonic presences within Anna: her father Jakob and her aunt Mina, who were both now in hell, along with Beelzebub, Judas and Lucifer. In addition, there were apparently a host of lesser demons fighting for attention. Over eight days, Riesinger did battle with them all as Anna screamed and thrashed about.

Then Riesinger confronted the demons head on. Beelzebub admitted having possessed Anna since she was 14 after Jakob had summoned him when Anna refused his advances. Jakob and Mina both confessed to wanting to ruin Anna, and Mina said she was a witch who had killed her own children. Judas said he had been brought forth to drive Anna to suicide.

At the final exorcism Riesinger claims to have seen each demon as it was driven out, including Lucifer.

It was on the fourth night that Anna suddenly collapsed back onto the bed. She opened her eyes, smiled and said, "My Jesus, Mercy! Praise be Jesus Christ!"

Anna went on to live a quiet life, and Father Riesinger enjoyed his celebrity. Jakob and Mina, as far as anyone knows, continue to live in hell.

OTHER
SUPERNATURAL
TALES

It is the nature of the supernatural and the occult not to fit into neat boxes. Sometimes stories are so strange that we can find no explanation at all, and even the occult categories we think we have nailed down are suddenly rent and torn.

Time travel, ESP, aliens – these encounters may be all of these things or none of them. Is this beast a ghost, a witch, a cryptid or is something else going on? Who are we going to call? The world of the paranormal is nothing if not inventive, and some of its inventions defy description, even by the most knowledgeable of paranormal investigators.

What is it about some places which brings forth unseen terrors, what is it about some moments in time that we feel there are gaps or where it seems to twist back on itself? And who are those people who make us think not once, not twice, but endlessly about what is going on beneath the surface of reality?

How do they appear, how do they disappear? Are they waiting for us on the other side, or is the other side right here where we are? These are the mysteries of the occult which not even the occult knows what to do with.

What can we do when we encounter the world that cannot be made rational? Should we fear it? It's impossible not to. Should we confront it? Not everyone has the strength. Do you?

OMENS

One power of witches is said to be that of necromancy, divining omens mere mortals cannot see. For those who hate surprises, the afterworld provides omens about when our time is up.

If you see a Headless Horseman, it's likely you won't see much else in this lifetime. Worse still, a disembodied arm might pierce the wall and push over your possessions, as allegedly happened in Scotland in the 1930s. A six-foot tall skeleton standing in your front garden is also a bad sign.

Some people have witnessed a procession of ghosts following the route of a future funeral – too bad if the funeral is yours. Best not to peek in the casket lest you see yourself.

Other omens are more difficult to divine. Seeing your own doppelgänger – a perfect replica of yourself – is seldom positive. Reputedly, doppelgängers are you in another dimension. Both ending up in the same one means accounts are being settled. You may also encounter corpse candles – floating balls of light. These will either hover around the doomed person or halfway between their home and the place they will be buried. Fishermen are especially vulnerable to these.

Sometimes your own actions bring on death. Opening an umbrella inside the house and holding it above your head is always trouble. Likewise lying down on a table – you'll be dead within a year. If you happen to be sewing, don't put your thimble down and then go and eat something. It is said to be fatal, like breaking a glass while making toast or three people looking in the same mirror at the same time. That's just common sense.

Animals, it is believed, can also be helpful in giving fair warning. A cat sleeping at the foot of your bed means death is close at hand, as does a rooster crowing in the dead of night. If you find a white moth in your house, then don't make any long-term plans, and it goes without saying that death-watch beetles are not your friends when it comes to living long. One in the furniture or tapping at the wall means death is just around the corner.

Also, it's best not to dream of either white horses or owls. In fact, dreams are a particularly fruitful realm when it comes to letting you know to order your burial plot. Dreams of absent loved ones paying a visit is a sure sign that they need to tell you something before you pop off. Snakes are a problem too, as are blackbirds. Some say that dreaming of a crying baby augurs no good, while the Indian holy book *The Ramayana* warns that any dream of swimming in cow dung may be your last.

As for dreams of dying, these mean one of two things. You may be seeing the future, in which case it's a bad sign. But many believe that dreams of death mean a transformation in your life, which may be a positive thing. So if you ever dream of falling off a cliff, being hit by a train or being murdered by a loved one, it really could go two ways. Half the fun is waiting.

THE BÉLMEZ FACES

On 23 August 1971, María Gómez Pereira was cooking in her kitchen in Bélmez, southern Spain, when something extraordinary happened. A dark stain spontaneously appeared in the middle of the concrete floor. Finding it unusual, but not unduly worried, she scrubbed it away and went on with her cooking.

When she turned around the stain was reappearing. Could it be a burst pipe under the floor? She and her husband Juan felt it, but it was not damp. María scrubbed it again and it came back.

Each day the stain grew a little more. After a week, María and Juan realized they were staring at a human face.

Disturbed by it, but still thinking it was a freak occurrence, Juan and his son Miguel decided to destroy the stain with pickaxes and re-lay the floor. A day passed, and then the stain re-appeared, grew and took form as a face.

Word spread. The mayor of Bélmez ordered the face be dug out and taken away to be studied. This was done, a new floor laid – and another face appeared. When they left this one, more faces appeared on other parts of the floor of men, women, children. Some faded and disappeared, others stayed. Men, women and children. Soon people were flocking to see the Faces of Bélmez.

Paranormal investigator Professor De Argumosa was called in. He was soon able to identify that the house may have been the site of an infamous seventeenth-century murder of five people. Were these the faces of the dead? But there were more than five.

Argumosa also noted that the family home was close to the church. Could the house have been built on top of the old cemetery? The mayor ordered the floor dug up and, sure enough, human remains were found, some dating back 700 years. It was decided that all the bones be dug up and reburied in the nearby Catholic cemetery. This was done, and the town went back about its business, with María and Juan getting a new floor, compliments of the mayor.

Then on 6 June 1972, as María Pereira sat in her kitchen – it happened again. Another face, same as the others. And another and another. By now some suspected fraud, so foil was placed over the floor to prevent the images being drawn by human hands. When they lifted the foil, there were more faces.

Paranormal investigators thought the faces were related to María's state of mind. When she was ill they seemed to fade a little. Could this be an instance of thoughtography, where an image is burned on a surface by thought alone? Could María have this power without knowing?

It was thought that when María died, this part of the conundrum might be solved. And when she did in February 2004 at the age of 85, no face appeared on the floor – for a few weeks. And then a small stain, growing bigger and gradually taking on the form of a human face. That of an elderly woman...

IS IT SO HARD TO TIDY UP AFTER YOURSELF?

Ever heard mysterious scratchings in the kitchen at night? Something in the cupboard or behind the stove? Obviously it could be a mouse or even a rat. Best get the exterminators in. Or maybe just keep things a little cleaner, especially as this may be no rodent at all. Worst case scenario, you may have a kikimora in the house.

First found in Japan, no one is quite sure what they look like – some think they have the snout of a pig, some that they resemble a goat or have the beak of a chicken. But all agree they have the body of a very thin woman and have straggly black hair. They wear a cloak of moss and never leave the house, lest they be blown away by the wind.

Where they come from is also a mystery. Some say they are the spirits of unbaptized babies, others that they are children who were cursed by their parents. Several have been identified living in houses built where a child was buried. Others say that they are planted in a house by the builders if they want to harm the family.

What is known for sure is that they like a well-ordered house. If the owners keep things clean, they will happily tend the chickens or spend their time weaving. There are even stories of them helping in the baking of bread or in lulling children to sleep.

But keep a slovenly house and the kikimora will exact a terrible price. They will scream in the night, break dishes and tip food on the floor. They can give you nightmares, and they have been known to climb onto a sleeper's chest and choke them to death. To prevent this one should turn one's pillow over just before sleeping and make the sign of a cross on it.

Children are particularly vulnerable to kikimora, either by being choked or kidnapped. Advise your child to always look out the window once – and only once – before they sleep as this pacifies the kikimora.

But the kitchen kikimora is not the only spirit to fear – there are also swamp kikimoras, who many believe are worse. They not only leap out of the darkness to frighten people, they have been known to grab them and drown them, strangers travelling in the night especially.

To tempt them to the swamp they are known to create lights on the surface which draw the traveller in, or to grow sweet-smelling plants on the water's edge to entice them. If this happens there is no escape – none have ever lived to tell the tale.

They have also been known to enter people's houses and steal their babies, leaving an enchanted log in the baby's place which will only reveal itself to be wood after a few days. Wet footprints in a child's bedroom can be a sign a swamp kikimora has visited. Mothers and fathers of small kids are always recommended to place a broom upside down behind the front door. It is believed the kikimora hates this.

But not every swamp kikimora is all bad. Legend tells of Baba Bolotnitsa, who brews beer at the swamp to draw the traveller to her. This is why on some nights the fog on a swamp is so thick – it is the steam of Baba Bolotnitsa brewing. While she may still kill you, survivors are known to make it home and declare that their drunkenness is not their fault, it is the doing of the swamp kikimora Baba Bolotnitsa.

THE BLACK DOG OF NEWGATE

As one might imagine, prisons have always been rich sources of supernatural lore. And when the prison is one of the busiest, in one of the busiest cities in the world, you can be sure there are plenty of unquiet souls to haunt it. While nobody knows exactly how many felons passed through London's Newgate Prison in its 700 years, we do know that 1,169 of them were executed. The executions took place just outside the walls, the crowds so vast that on one occasion in 1807, 12 bystanders lost their lives in a crush of 40,000 spectators.

But it was a prisoner who didn't make it to the gallows whose legend still haunts Newgate. In 1596, a young scholar named Luke Sutton told the tale of another scholar, named Schoiler, jailed for sorcery. It was during the famine in the reign of Henry III, and the inmates of the jail had already resorted to cannibalism when Schoiler arrived. His magic powers afforded him no protection – they quickly descended on him and ate him. But as he died he vowed to have his revenge for this most awful of deaths. The deaths of his killers would be far, far worse.

Shortly afterwards, the prisoners reported seeing a monstrous coal-black dog walking the corridors of Newgate. The dog would sniff out the murderers of the sorcerer and consume them in turn, eating them alive in front of their fellow inmates. The rumour spread that this was the spirit of the dead man, come back to take vengeance. Those it did not kill often killed themselves to avoid their fate, while one escaped and told the story to Luke Sutton. Later, according to Sutton, even the escapee was found and devoured by the Black Dog of Newgate.

The death of the last killer, however, does not seem to have sated the dog's appetite, and Newgate never got free of its malign presence. Until the jail was closed in 1902, frightened prisoners would report seeing its shadow moving through the corridors, and more than one reported hearing it shredding a fellow inmate at night.

Some say that this is not the spirit of the sorcerer, but a nearby ghost taking canine shape. The ghost of Amen Court – which shared a wall with Newgate graveyard – is said to be an amorphous black mass which haunts the street between the prison and St Paul's Cathedral.

Some believe this to be the ghost of Amelia Dyer, the Victorian mass murderer known as the Baby Farmer for killing children in the Thames – 400, according to some reports, which would make her the most prolific serial killer in history. Some even think she may have been Jack the Ripper. But she was executed at Newgate in 1896, so the dates don't work out for her to be related to the Black Dog, unless the Black Dog saw a way to transfer itself out of Newgate and find more victims. Stranger things have happened.

As for Luke Sutton, rumour had it he may have been the youngest son of the Archbishop of York and like the man in his tale, he was said to have dabbled in sorcery, perhaps was even a warlock. He was, it was said, "so valiant that he feared not men nor Laws". The law he should have feared was that for robbery. He was caught in 1598 and executed at York – the Archbishop deciding, they say, not to intervene and save his evil son.

JIANGSHI

On first inspection some of them look like normal humans, but on closer inspection there are signs of death. Usually, however, the flesh is already decomposing, and those who have encountered them and lived often tell of them being pale white but with mould or moss growing on them. Their name meaning "stiff corpse", the Jiangshi are the infamous zombie vampires of China.

They were first identified in the late eighteenth century, but accounts differ as to their origin. Some believe that they are the bodies of the dead who failed to get a proper burial, and then when lightning struck them or a cat leapt across their coffins they were reanimated. Or they could be people who died and whose souls failed leave their bodies, their death was improper or they committed suicide. Trapped inside the dead bodies, the souls can only survive by feeding on the souls of the living.

Being dead, the Jiangshi are completely stiff, and so they need to bounce on two feet to move around, their arms outstretched before them. But do not be fooled into thinking this makes them easy to get away from. Once a Jiangshi has you in its sights, there is very little you can do.

Some say they suck blood, but experts deny this, believing

this to be a later confusion with Western vampires. Unlike vampires, the Jiangshi have no intelligence – they kill to take souls and nothing more. One cannot reason with a Jiangshi. And they say that few deaths are as horrific – to get the soul the Jiangshi will literally tear a human to pieces. They can grow long claws for exactly this purpose.

It is also said that with each soul the Jiangshi grows stronger and may even acquire the power of transformation, such as turning into a wolf. That said, the Jiangshi can do more damage than a wolf, so it seems unlikely they would change. They may be able to fly.

There are, according to legend, certain ways to prepare for a Jiangshi attack. They are, it is said, appalled by their own reflections, so always carry a mirror. It is also said that they can't go near money without stopping to count it, so throwing cash on the ground may keep you safe for a time – the more money the longer it will take them.

Other defence options, such as the wood of a peach tree, vinegar and a black donkey's hooves seem unlikely to do the trick, although some swear by them. A more plausible weapon seems to be the blood of a black dog, which can be hurled at a Jiangshi to repel it (some say to touch it to their forehead, but getting this close seems risky). Or you could use a sword fashioned in the light of a full moon.

There are also those who say holding your breath can work. Looking for a living soul, the Jiangshi will be fooled into thinking you are dead, or perhaps they can't identify a soul when it has no access to air? Whether the Jiangshi will be instantly fooled and move on or wait things out a while is not known, which suggests those who have tried it did not live to tell.

But there is hope. Some say that if it eats enough souls the Jiangshi will come back to life. And one less Jiangshi is never a bad thing.

HOIA BACIU FOREST

Transylvania. The home of Count Dracula, the most iconic of all vampires. But if you want to know true fear, visit Hoia Baciu Forest, the most supernatural place, locals will tell you, in the whole world.

Entering the forest can give the most hardened paranormal investigator the heebie-jeebies. Eerily quiet, Hoia Baciu's warped and contorted trees seem to reach out to you. Scientists cannot explain why the trees grow the way they do, twisted rather than straight, and always in a clockwise direction. Are there supernatural forces acting on them, pulling them in these directions?

Stand still and you might hear soft footsteps on wet leaves in the distance, despite no one being there. There is no bird song.

Locals say that once you enter the forest, you must confront your own deepest fears. Visitors experience strange headaches and nausea. Some have even found burn marks on their skin or developed rashes – until they finally leave the forest.

If you had been here in the 1960s, you might have seen some of the mysterious figures photographed by the biologist Alexandru Sift. He captured shadows that seemed to be following him, emerging from behind trees and disappearing again. When he had the photos developed, they came out in a different order.

Or you might have seen the photograph by military technician Emil Barnea which ufologists have called "one of the clearest photos of a UFO ever taken in Romania and, without doubt, one of the best images of its kind, in the entire world". The place where he took the photograph is called the "dead zone", a perfect circle where no vegetation grows. Did aliens land on the spot?

But even before this visitation, locals would tell the story of the Shepherd of Hoia Baciu Forest. They say that one day a local shepherd was having trouble finding pasture for his sheep. All his life he had avoided the forest, as all the other shepherds warned him not to go there.

Finally, he decided that the stories were all a fantasy – what could possibly go wrong. Saying goodbye to his wife, he released his sheepdogs and led his flock across the hills and into the forest. No one knows if it was ghosts, or aliens, or something in between, perhaps the forest itself, but neither he, nor the sheepdogs, nor the 200 sheep, were ever seen again.

Most locals believe that he may have fallen into a vortex, or a parallel universe. If so, he might still come back. After all, only recently a five-year-old girl disappeared in the forest and everyone had given up on ever seeing her alive again. Then five years later she walked out of the forest, still dressed exactly the same, still a five-year-old-girl. But even if he does, perhaps like her he won't think he has been gone for more than a moment, and his sheep will still have lambs at foot.

So if you ever find yourself in Transylvania, leave Dracula's castle to the tourists. Take a trip into the Hoia Baciu Forest. We'll see you in a few years' time…

THE MOBERLY–JOURDAIN INCIDENT

It's a question many of us have pondered. If you could return to any time in history, when would it be? Everyone will have their own answer, but an inconvenient lack of time machines has meant that it has all remained very hypothetical.

If your answer is something like the palace of the most magnificent king in history, Louis XIV, then it's possible you might be interested to know that time travel has, allegedly, already been achieved, over 100 years ago.

In 1911, two women, Charlotte Moberly and Eleanor Jourdain, were on a tour of the Palace of Versailles, where Louis had his court two centuries before. Both were teachers of high standing at an exclusive school in England.

Bored with the tour they struck out alone and got lost somewhere between the Grand Trianon Park and the Petite Trianon, the small house in the grounds which famously housed Louis XVI's wife, Marie Antoinette.

Suddenly the two women felt very oppressed. There were people around them in eighteenth-century dress: cloaks, three-cornered hats and the like. They anxiously asked a blonde woman in a richly tapestried dress who was lying on the grass sketching for advice on how to get out of Versailles. The woman did not answer, she just continued her sketch. They could see her hands were shaking.

As the two women recounted, trees grew flat and two-dimensional, "like wood worked into tapestry". No wind stirred where it had before, and there were no effects of light and shade. They felt like they were in a painting, although they could still move around. It was, they said, "unnatural" and "sinister".

Worse, they passed a cottage where a woman was handing a jug to a girl in the doorway. Both of them were frozen; the water from the jug spilling over the side did not move either.

Then they saw a sight which horrified them even further. There was a man seated in the garden in a cloak and hat. As they walked, "The man slowly turned his face... The expression was evil and yet unseeing..."

Finally the women found their tour and rejoined it. Shaken, they did not even speak about their experiences to each other until about a week later. They felt they needed to go back to Versailles to try and find the place where they had been.

Try as they might, they could not. They took notes about what they had seen that day and sketched the places they had been. One particular thing was missing: a small bridge they had crossed, which had been removed at some point. From this and other clues they were able to guess the date that they may have been in Versailles. It matched contemporary accounts of 10 August 1792. Six weeks before the revolution which ended the monarchy.

Was this why they felt such a sense of oppression? Had all of those they encountered been doomed? It has long been believed that those who will die soon can feel a sense of dread, which can be communicated unconsciously to those around them.

And what of the young woman sketching? The two women compared notes and examined portraits. They were now certain of who she was, and why her hands were shaking. In just a short while, Marie Antoinette would be dead.

THE MAN FROM TAURED

Of course, hopping through time and space dimensions may not only be a talent held by humans. It is possible that it is a talent shared with other creatures, even some very much like ourselves.

In 1954, a Caucasian man arrived at Haneda Airport in Tokyo, Japan, carrying a briefcase. As he made his way through customs, an official noticed his passport looked odd. "Would you answer some questions, sir?" he asked. "Of course, no problem," replied the man.

He told the official that this was his third visit to Japan that year, and though his primary language was French, he spoke fluent Japanese, as well as three other languages. He was well travelled, and in his wallet were various European currencies. "That's fine, thank you, sir, but may we ask you where you are actually from?" "Yes," he replied. "I am from Taured."

Sure enough, his passport confirmed he was from Taured, which he said was between France and Spain. Asked by the baffled officials to point to it on a map, he grew confused, as he could not find it either. Nor was the company he said he was dealing with aware of his existence, while the hotel he mentioned had no bookings for him, nor did they know his name. This despite him having a number of documents to say he had frequently done business in Japan and stayed at the same hotel.

Clearly agitated, the man seemed to think the officials were playing a trick on him, even more so when they again showed him a map and there was a country called "Andorra" where his homeland of Taured was supposed to be. Now he grew irate and started to tell the officials of the rich history of Taured, which surely they knew?

With both parties completely confused, the customs officials decided the best thing to do would be to put the man up in a hotel for the night while they ran a series of checks on his extremely convincing documents. The man agreed. He was still upset but would wait patiently until the whole thing was sorted out. They would, they informed him, have to set a guard outside his door, as without a valid passport he was technically an illegal alien. He agreed – what else could he do?

The next morning the officials greeted the guard and knocked on the man's door. No response. They tried again. Still the same. Eventually they obtained a master key and let themselves in. The man from Taured was gone. The officials phoned their office to get the documents taken from the safe and sent over. They were gone too. It was as if the man from Taured had never existed.

Or had he? Some have claimed that the man from Taured was an accidental visitor from another part of the universe, exactly like ours in many ways, but subtly different in others. Might he have somehow passed through some sort of portal and come out in our world, genuinely being as baffled as the officials who tried to deal with the case?

Which also of course leaves a deeper question – was there a man from Andorra who was on his third visit that year to

Japan being asked by a group of officials somewhere in a parallel universe to point to Andorra on a map and only seeing Taured? Did he talk of Andorra's rich history to baffled customs officers? Did he mysteriously disappear the next morning and return to our world? And if so, did he make his meeting?

THE BROMPTON
TIME MACHINE

There have, of course, been many attempts to discover the occult science of time travel. In the 1960s, Vatican scientist-priest Father Pellegrino Ernetti claimed to have achieved it with what he called a Chronovisor. The machine was said to allow viewers to watch events from the past, including speeches by the Roman senator Cicero, Napoleon and Mussolini.

Ernetti also produced a picture of the crucifixion of Jesus to, he hoped, prove that both Christ and the Chronovisor were real. The image turned out to have been taken from a postcard of a mural of Christ in a church in Italy, cunningly reversed. Despite this suspicion of hoax, some say the machine remains hidden away in the Vatican.

But there is a more promising example of what many believe to be an authentic time machine. In the middle of Brompton Cemetery, England stands a tall mausoleum which towers above the graves around it. In it lies the body of Hannah Courtoy (1784–1849) and, according to some reports, the secret of time travel.

Like many Victorians, Courtoy was obsessed with Ancient Egypt and decided that her resting place should mimic an

Egyptian burial tomb. Designed by Joseph Bonomi and Samuel Alfred Warner, it features a number of hieroglyphics. Bonomi was an expert in Egyptology while Warner was an inventor, who claimed to have created a "high explosive underwater mine or torpedo no bigger than a duck's egg", some feat in 1830. Tests staged to capture the interest of King William IV which involved dropping it from a hot air balloon were inconclusive.

Rumour has it that Bonomi had deciphered the secret to time travel from hieroglyphics and convinced Courtoy to finance his work with Warner on building the first such contraption. They are said to have theorized that by putting it in a cemetery it would be safe from prying eyes. Also, cemeteries seldom change – their time machine would be hidden in plain sight for many centuries.

On Hannah Courtoy's death the two men fashioned the mausoleum. Aside from the hieroglyphics, it has wheel motifs and a place where a clock might fit. Unlike every other structure in Brompton cemetery, no architect's plans for it exist. Neither, mysteriously, does a key – it is said to have disappeared one night five years after Courtoy's death.

Also five years after her death, Samuel Alfred Warner died in mysterious circumstances. He is buried in Brompton, in an unmarked grave. Some say Bonomi killed him to stop him revealing the secrets of the machine. Others say that the shock of what he saw while travelling through space and time did him in. There are others who say he never died at all but left for other realms, taking the key with him.

Bonomi lived another 20 years, continuing to design buildings, publish studies of Egypt and inventing a machine for accurately measuring the proportions of the human body.

He visited the mausoleum often and could be seen attempting to gain access on more than one occasion.

When he died he was buried close to the mausoleum. His tomb features an illustration of Anubis, the Egyptian god of death, mummification, embalming, tombs, cemeteries and the afterlife. Anubis faces towards Courtoy's mausoleum. Is Joseph Bonomi still hoping that Samuel Alfred Warner will return one day and take him on the journey he always dreamed of?

POVEGLIA

In 2014, the lease to a small island off the coast of Venice was auctioned by the Italian state. While the government would keep outright ownership, they were looking for someone to redevelop the hospital on the island into a luxury resort and share the profits with them. Sounds like easy money.

However, there were no takers, because this was no ordinary island. This was Poveglia, believed by many to be the most terrifying place on Earth.

First mentioned in documentation dating back to 421 CE, Poveglia was so exposed that when the Genoans attacked Venice in 1379, the inhabitants were taken to safety on the mainland and the island left deserted. Then the plague struck.

The Venetians sent their sick to Poveglia and those who had already died of the disease would be thrown into giant pits, known as "Poveglian pits". When each pit was full it was covered with dirt and set on fire. Some claim that Poveglia is 50 per cent ash and 50 per cent human bones.

Macabre rumours started to spread. It had been noticed that any time a death pit was disturbed, some of the freshly dead had blood coming out of their mouths. Many thought these were vampires feeding on the other dead, and so stones were placed in the mouths of all the corpses to stop them biting.

We now know that this was the effect of decomposition gasses in the corpses, which would explode internal organs.

Around 160,000 plague victims were buried on Poveglia, and fishermen still find skulls in their catch, no matter how much they avoid going close to the island. Some claim that on calm nights you can still hear the victims screaming.

But that wasn't the end of the horrors of Poveglia. In 1922, with the plague long passed, the hospital on the island was turned into an asylum for psychiatric patients. Unfortunately the doctor put in charge was himself unstable – perhaps the island turned him that way – and he started to carry out terrible experiments on the patients. Like lobotomies using a chisel and hammer.

Eventually the doctor himself went completely mad and threw himself off the tallest tower in the hospital. It is said that he was driven to do so by the ghosts of those he had killed. Perhaps it was them that ensured he didn't die when he hit the ground but was left to suffer in the enveloping mists. Another victim of Poveglia.

Other inmates of the asylum are said to haunt the island – Pietro, whose legs were amputated and whose wheelchair can be heard going up and down the corridors, and Frederico, who laughs all day and night. Other faces are seen at the windows by fishermen, including a young girl with terrified eyes and a chisel hole on her forehead.

Perhaps one day they will build a luxury hotel on the island and the curse of Poveglia will finally be lifted. It might be that the undead who haunt the island would be happy to see a bunch of pleasure seekers join them for a relaxing holiday. What do you think?

GRIM UP NORTH

The story goes like this. One day a group of villagers in North Yorkshire, England, decided to build a bridge. Unfortunately, their chosen spot was continually battered by floodwaters and no bridge they could build would withstand them. The Devil appeared and promised that he would erect one in exchange for one soul – belonging to whoever crossed the bridge first.

The villagers agreed and watched as the Devil constructed the bridge quickly. The floodwaters were weak against the robust edifice. "You see my power," said the Devil and demanded his prize.

The villagers could not decide who should make the first trip. The Devil became impatient and threatened to destroy the bridge as fast as he'd made it. Then one villager, with his faithful dog Grim, stepped forward and said that as sad as it made him, he would make the terrible sacrifice.

He walked to the edge of the bridge and then suddenly dived into the water, swimming to the other side of the river and climbing out at the other end of the bridge. "You see, Devil," he said, "I hereby make the terrible sacrifice." He then called for Grim, who ran across the bridge and whose soul became the Devil's.

It is not known if the Devil kept the dog, or just stamped

his foot and disappeared (as he did in Regensburg, Germany in similar circumstances – you can still see the bump where he stamped), but it is not the last we hear of Grim in the world of demons.

In some English villages it was deemed vital to bury a dog alive under the cornerstones of the church to guard the dead from thieves, witches and even the Devil. These are "church grims", perhaps named for the brave dog who was sacrificed on the bridge.

It is said they can change their form, and if you hear the church bell toll just before midnight it is the grim announcing an imminent death. The grim can also be seen looking out of the church tower after a body is buried, to see if the soul is ascending to heaven.

In Scandinavia a similar tradition is followed, although lambs, boars, pigs or dogs may be used. They also protect the dead and the sacred building itself, but if it appears while a gravedigger is at work then soon a child will die.

But there is one place that needs no grim, and that is Myanmar. There the graves are protected by a determined woman named Ma Phae Wah, which means "the yellow ribbon lady", named for the ribbon she wears in her hair

Unlike the grims she does not just protect the dead, she actively goes out and increases their number. Each midnight she hoists an empty coffin on her shoulder and moves through the village. She chooses a house and places the coffin on the doorstep. Then she returns to the grave and waits for someone in the family, usually a child, to sicken and die and be placed in the casket. She never has to wait long.

Some say she eats the babies, but in the 1990s a Buddhist monk reported that he had a dream where he had convinced

Ma Phae Wah that, rather than eating children, she should eat the dogs which prowled around the graveyard instead. It is said that since then, she only has an appetite for canine flesh.

Poor Grim!

CARL AND ELENA

According to everyone else in the world except one, there is nothing paranormal about the love Carl Tanzler shared with Elena de Hoyos. That one person is Carl Tanzler.

A German, Tanzler claimed descent from the Countess of Cosel, the eighteenth-century mistress of the King of Poland, whose ghost Tanzler claimed visited him as a child. Although well travelled, Tanzler otherwise lived a humble life, marrying Doris Schafer in 1920 and having two children. In 1926, he emigrated to the United States to join his sister and became a radiologist in Florida. His wife and children were to follow later.

On 22 April 1930, a beautiful 22-year-old Cuban-American came into the hospital where he was working. Later he would claim that she was exactly the woman he had been having visions of all his life. To say he fell head over heels is an understatement. She became his great obsession. But Maria Elena Milagro de Hoyos had a fatal problem – she had tuberculosis.

Tanzler left his wife and children and showered Elena with gifts, jewellery and perfume, but there is no record of her responding. Despite his best efforts, his love died on 25 October 1931 at her parents' house. Tanzler insisted on paying for the funeral and building a large mausoleum for her, which he then visited every night. He said she sang to him in Spanish and finally declared her love for him.

The death of one's beloved is normally the end of the romance. But not for Tanzler. One night in April 1933, he heard Maria ask him to take her home. He removed her body from the mausoleum and he carted her away on a toy wagon to his home.

For the next seven years he lived with Elena as his wife, in a chilling sense. He held the body together with piano wire, filled her chest and abdomen with rags for her to retain her shapely figure, fitted her with glass eyes and used perfume and disinfectant to mask the smell of her decomposing body. As her flesh fell off he replaced it with plaster of Paris.

His sister was the first to discover that Tanzler had Elena with him – before then people had seen him through the window dancing with her and assumed she was still alive. She notified the authorities and Tanzler was arrested in October 1940 on a charge of "wantonly and maliciously destroying a grave and removing a body without authorization". But perhaps Elena intervened from the afterlife – or he was just the beneficiary of good fortune – as the crime had just passed the statute of limitations for conviction. The time limit for conviction had passed and Tanzler walked free.

So sensational was the case that Elena's body was put on display at the Dean-Lopez Funeral Home. Over 7,000 people came to look at her, before she was returned to Key West cemetery.

As for Tanzler? Deprived of his love he did the next best thing. He created a life-size doll of her, using her death mask to ensure it had the exact features of his love. For the next 12 years they continued to live as husband and wife, and he could again be seen dancing at the window with her.

He died on 3 July 1952, at the age of 75. Elena would have been 43, but to him she would always be 22. His body was not found for three weeks after he died, but it is said that he was still in Elena's arms. Some say that he had managed to swap the doll for her real body, and it was the true Elena he died with. But that would be just too weird.

THE TWINS

Originally from Barbados, twins June and Jennifer were destined to be outcasts in a Welsh town where they were the only Black children.

There is evidence showing that twins share a special bond and can communicate almost telepathically. Some see this as proof of the paranormal trespassing into everyday life. But June and Jennifer seemed to take this a step further.

From the time they could first talk, the girls spoke of switching selves – June would become Jennifer and Jennifer would become June, constantly bouncing backwards and forwards between each other's bodies. Sometimes it seemed both girls inhabited one body – either June or Jennifer would talk to themselves while the other sat silently.

Gradually they began to withdraw from the world. They wouldn't talk to anyone else, including their parents. When they spoke to each other it was in their own invented language, a mixture of Barbadian and English, a sped-up Bajan Creole.

Their parents took them to a therapist, who recommended sending the girls to separate boarding schools. This made things worse, for not only did they still not talk to anyone, they both became catatonic, not speaking or moving.

When together, they retreated to their rooms and invented a whole universe for their dolls. When a doll died, it was recorded in a notebook, which even gave a cause of death. That doll was no longer played with.

At 16 they were loners, seeing only each other and sometimes their younger sister, Rosie, for whom they would make tapes of their stories. Rosie bought them diaries, in which the twins wrote more stories. Later they took a mail order course in creative writing. Both wrote novels about bad and criminal men and women. June's novel *The Pepsi-Cola Addict* about a young boy seduced by his teacher has been published a number of times.

But in their diaries they also recorded their increasingly hostile feelings towards each other. Jennifer wrote, "We have become fatal enemies in each other's eyes... I say to myself, can I get rid of my own shadow, impossible or not possible? Without my shadow, would I die? Without my shadow, would I gain life, be free or left to die?" and June, "She wants us to be equal. There is a murderous gleam in her eye. Dear lord, I am scared of her. She is not normal ... someone is driving her insane. It is me."

In 1981, now 18 and using drugs and alcohol, the girls ended up in jail for a series of petty thefts and arson. Inside they came to agreement that one of them would have to die for the other to be free, and that the survivor would then speak to others and live a normal life. After 11 years inside, under constant watch, the girls were released from prison and sent to a hospital with less surveillance.

That very night, Jennifer Gibbons died. The cause was an undiagnosed heart infection. But had the girls carried out their pact by supernatural means? Was Jennifer merely fulfilling her side of the pact? June said, "I'm free at last, liberated, and at last Jennifer has given up her life for me." She now lives in Wales near her parents, a normal member of the community.

HOOKMAN

They say it is an urban legend, but who can be sure? He seems to have struck many times, and always the story is the same. Well, more or less. He seems to have quietened down a little now that teenagers spend less time "making out" in cars. But perhaps he is just biding his time. After all, if you are an immortal half-man half-beast like Hookman, you have all the time in the world.

It was in a popular US newspaper advice column that he first came to notice. One dark night in 1950s Detroit, Jeanette and her date were in their car doing a little "necking". The music they were listening to on the radio, perhaps a little Buddy Holly or some Ritchie Valens, was suddenly interrupted by a news announcement. A convict had escaped from the local jail and was being pursued by police. People should stay away from him as he was extremely dangerous. He had one distinguishing feature – a hook for a hand.

The teenagers were a little frightened and the boyfriend took a moment to reassure Jeanette that they were safe. The music started playing once more, and next thing they were necking again.

Suddenly there was a loud bang on Jeanette's door. The kids tried to see what it was, but it was too dark. Fumbling for the keys, her date managed to get the car started and hit the accelerator just as there was a second loud bang. As he tore off, the two teenagers heard a loud scream but did not look back.

When they got to Jeanette's house, they sat there shaking. But as was the custom, the date got out of his door and went round to her side of the car. There, stuck in the passenger side door, was a giant hook. As Jeanette said in her letter, "I will never park to make out as long as I live. I hope this does the same for other kids."

But other kids failed to take Jeanette's advice. Across America there was a spate of attacks by Hookman, who obviously had an endless supply of hooks. Sometimes rather than banging the car door he would tease the occupants by scraping at it; sometimes rather than going for the door he climbed on the roof, with the terrified teenagers grabbing each other as the shiny hook burst through the ceiling.

Some teenagers managed to hit the accelerator and drive off swerving, throwing Hookman off. But either others weren't so lucky, or Hookman was getting smarter and not advertising his presence before striking. Urban legend has it that in some cases he was even smart enough to stand in the distance being creepy, and then when the boy came out to confront him, he seemed to disappear, only for the boy to return to the car and find his date murdered.

Or the boy wouldn't come back, and the girl would go to look for him, only to find his mutilated body, sometimes attached to a tree by the hook, sometimes attached to the car. If she was lucky, that was the end of it, but sometimes he killed her too. Spare hook!

Worst of all, the car would break down and the boy would go to look for help. She would lock the doors and fall asleep.

When she woke up, a terrifying stranger would be staring through the window. In one hand he had the car keys, and on his hook the severed head of her boyfriend. Her fate is unknown but can be guessed.

Jeanette did try to warn them!

LIGHTS ON, LIGHTS OFF

Ask most people about parapsychology, the study of such things as ESP, telepathy and clairvoyance, and they will tend to be sceptical or talk about those with some sort of superpowers or occult training. But there is one phenomenon which more and more people are experiencing – some of whom include the very sceptics who write of occult experiences, and those who think their magical powers are unlikely to exist.

A short while ago – in cosmic terms anyway – people started noticing something very odd happening, particularly in cities. As they were walking along, streetlights they passed under would go out. It seemed so mundane that most barely gave it a thought, or believed it a coincidence, perhaps just some little party trick they could occasionally do.

But as the incidents mounted, and the number of people with this potential ability grew, parapsychologists were able to identify a new and fascinating phenomenon: "Street Light Interference" syndrome, commonly known as SLI. Those with the alleged capacity became known as SLIders.

So what is going on here? Some scientists were still happy to put things down to the coincidence theory. Given all the streetlights in the world, and all the people walking under them, there will always be one going off above someone somewhere.

Furthermore, people are far more likely to notice a streetlight going off than one that stays on.

Moreover, engineers pointed to a failure mode that streetlights at the end of their life have called "cycling", which means they turn on and off more frequently. This, however, only happens with older models of streetlights, not newer ones, of which there are many more.

Researchers have shown that the electronic impulses in the brain may be the answer to the question. The effects of these impulses on the body have been explored and are now acknowledged as science fact. But what of their effect on the world around them?

One of the intriguing things about SLIders is that they often claim to be in an extreme emotional state when they put out streetlights. Could it be that their brains are "firing on all cylinders" and this makes their electrical impulses more likely to affect outside objects?

Some SLIders report other electrical objects around them also suffering interference when they are agitated, like radios developing static, televisions and lamps turning on and off, watches stopping again and again, even credit cards with magnetic strips not working.

Because the power of SLIders is usually out of their control, it has been very hard to study the phenomenon in the laboratory. It is difficult to do a controlled experiment with someone who can't control what they are doing.

And yet the number of people who are experiencing SLI continues to grow. Some have speculated that as our lives become more and more dependent on electrical items, from laptops to mobile phones and even electric cars, the increase in static electricity may also be increasing the electrical impulses in our brains. And one could argue, they are certainly making us more stressed, which might be making things even worse.

But is it a new phenomenon? Way back in 1837, an American woman found herself charged up with electricity for five months, so anyone she touched got a shock. That was only two years after the first ever constant electric light was displayed at a public meeting. The inventor pointed out he could "read a book at a distance of one and a half feet". They say that the moment he said this, the bulb went out...

SKULDUGGERY?

He was one of America's greatest writers and poets. He was also a brilliant satirist, and his war stories influenced future scribes such as Ernest Hemingway. Many were the strings to Ambrose Bierce's bow. Including horror stories.

But when Bierce left the US in 1913 to report on the Mexican Revolution, he was going as a journalist. Although 71, he was in pretty robust health apart from asthma, and his friends, family and all of America waited with some excitement to see what he would make of the conflagration south of the border.

He was never heard from again.

We know he went first to visit some American Civil War battlefields and that he had passed through Texas. He was rumoured to have been at the Battle of Tierra Blanca, which took place in late November. And on the day after Christmas he wrote to his friend, fellow journalist Blanche Partington, finishing the letter by saying, "As to me, I leave here tomorrow for an unknown destination." The destination remains unknown.

Investigations began – as one of America's most famous writers his disappearance was front page news. Partington was unable to produce the actual letter, just her own quote from it in her notebook. Some thought the pair may have had a secret agreement to fool everyone, and that Bierce had decided to commit suicide – a few years before his two sons had predeceased him, leaving him depressed. Also, suicidal writers captured the American imagination.

Perhaps Bierce and Partington had cooked the whole thing up and there was no trip to Mexico.

Others noted one of his final letters to his publisher: "Goodbye. If you hear of my being stood up against a Mexican stone wall and shot to rags, please know that I think it is a pretty good way to depart this life. It beats old age, disease, or falling down the cellar stairs. To be a Gringo in Mexico – ah, that is euthanasia!" Had he in fact been shot by firing squad, his details lost in the fog of war?

But there is another theory – that Bierce had gone to Mexico not alone but with a man called F. A. Mitchell-Hedges in search of the legendary Crystal Skull. This was said to be an artefact from pre-Columbian times which allowed people to see into both the past and the future. He and Bierce corresponded, and Mitchell-Hedges in his extensive name-dropping autobiography claimed to have found one of the skulls in Mexico... in 1913.

That he didn't mention Bierce in his autobiography seems odd. Bierce, the horror writer, had even corresponded with Mitchell-Hedges about it. So why the silence?

Did both men go seeking the skull? Did Bierce die on the way there or on the way back? Of natural causes? Or... unnatural ones?

We will never know – when Mitchell-Hedges died the skull was never found. Perhaps the gods had reclaimed it. But recently another letter of Bierce's was uncovered. He said he was going to Mexico not to report the war, but for a reason "not at present disclosable".

A case of skulduggery?

THE HUMAN PILLARS

Many people are familiar with the Catacombs in Paris. Go beneath the city streets and you will find the bones of six million dead arranged in beautiful patterns by the workers tasked with moving them from the city's overflowing cemeteries in the eighteenth century.

But in Hokkaido, Japan, in the 1960s, a much stranger discovery was made. After an earthquake hit, rescue workers were looking for survivors in a railway tunnel. They found something gruesome.

Breaking open a wall, they discovered a long line of human skeletons, standing to attention side by side. The skeletons had been used as human pillars, supporting the wall, which had been built 50 years earlier.

Sealing people inside walls or even bridges has a long history, either as punishment or to appease the gods, so whoever had done this was following an old tradition. But it had long been felt it was an ancient custom, not the sort of thing you would expect to find in a place like Hokkaido.

Afterwards the tunnel, as with the rest of the city, was rebuilt. As far as anyone knows, this time concrete was used!

HORSE IS A HORSE

His name was Snippy, a three-year-old Appaloosa horse, and one day in 1967 he had failed to return to the Harry King Ranch in Alamosa, Colorado, where he was stabled. Agnes King and her son Harry went to look for him. What they found was horrifying and would be the first in a series of bizarre livestock mutilations that continue throughout the world to this day.

Snippy's head and neck had been skinned, his flesh removed neatly. No blood was found, just a medicinal smell. Nor were there any footmarks around the dead horse except those of Agnes and Harry, but there were scorch marks on the ground. One hundred yards away was a flattened bush and six indentations in a circle.

While an investigation found that "There is no evidence to support the assertion that the horse's death was associated in any way to abnormal causes", rumours spread about a madman, an ant attack or aliens. The latter seemed to explain the lack of footmarks and perhaps the scorch marks. Snippy passed into local legend, but the world lost interest.

Then in 1973, a wave of cattle mutilations swept across Nebraska and Kansas, 38 in total. While what happened to them differed from what happened to Snippy, there were some shared elements, including how methodical the attacks were and the lack of any footprints left by the attackers.

The mutilations increased. A senator contacted the FBI to investigate as there had been about 130 mutilations in his state of Colorado alone. There were reports of other forms of other attacks elsewhere. As with Snippy, blood was taken, but also organs, eyes, tongues. Some of the animals had most of their bones broken, like they had been dropped from a great height.

On 20 August 1974, the *Lincoln Journal Star* reported that in places where mutilations had occurred, eerie lights like those of helicopters had been seen. The government said that no helicopters were known to be in the air at the time.

Was this some sort of cult activity? The taking of organs and blood seemed to suggest it as a possibility if they were being taken for satanic rituals. But the scale of the mutilations and the precision of the injuries made this seem unlikely, although some cults may have jumped on the bandwagon.

Government experiments? Here the volume of deaths and their precision made things more likely. These experiments might have been malign, to explore future possibilities for human experimentation, or more benign, to track the spread of bovine diseases, and the possibility of them being transmitted to humans.

But how could such research be kept secret? Those sorts of findings would only be useful if they led to possible disease control and prevention, which would need to be explained.

Which leaves aliens. Could it be that the blood and organs of these animals would be somehow useful to extra-terrestrials in a way that their meat is not? It would explain the bright lights in the sky, the lack of tracks on the ground and the strange non-human use of beasts which were bred as human food.

To human carnivores, they seemed to be throwing away the best bit.

The mutilations continue to this day, mostly in the Americas and Australia. It is estimated that only one in ten incidents ever gets reported, which means hundreds of thousands of deaths so far.

As for Snippy? His remains were put up for auction on eBay in 2006 but failed to reach the reserve price of $50,000. He is now rumoured to be in a warehouse in Denver.

THE INVENTOR

If you ever want to feel bad about what you've achieved in life, just compare yourself with Thomas Edison. He invented the phonograph. He invented the motion picture camera. He invented the lightbulb. That enough? How about the rechargeable battery? The radiograph? Infra-red sensors – he didn't even patent that one, thinking there wouldn't be a market. Just did it in his spare time. Basically, if you are in a lit room, or watching a screen, or listening to music, you are using one of Edison's inventions.

BUT if you want to feel better about yourself, then best focus on his last invention, the Spirit Phone. Edison believed that it should be possible to communicate with the dead – by scientific means. While a man of science, he believed in God as well – "I can no more doubt the existence of an Intelligence that is running things," he said, "than I do the existence of myself."

He believed that all living bodies were made up of "myriads and myriads of infinitesimally small individuals, each in itself a unit of life", and that those units of life, which worked in "swarms", were everlasting. When a person dies, these swarms would then take form elsewhere, in a different place, environment or vessel.

"If the units of life which compose an individual's memory hold together after that individual's death," Edison reasoned, "is it not within range of possibility... that the individual's memory, or personality, ought to be able to function as before."

Therefore, "I have been at work for some time building an apparatus to see if it is possible for personalities which have left this earth to communicate with us," Edison said. "If this is ever accomplished it will be accomplished not by any occult, mystifying, mysterious or weird means, such as are employed by so-called mediums, but by scientific methods."

It is believed that Edison carried out a demonstration of his machine for a select group of scientists in a secret laboratory, but he was continuing to tweak his invention right up until his own swarms departed his life.

Two years later, in 1933, *Modern Mechanix* magazine published details of the earlier trial. "Edison set up a photo-electric cell. A tiny pencil of light, coming from a powerful lamp, bored through the darkness and struck the active surface of this cell, where it was transformed instantly into a feeble electric current. Any object, no matter how thin, transparent or small, would cause a registration on the cell if it cut through the beam."

Impressed, the scientist watched... and watched... and watched. Nothing happened.

Which is not to say it wouldn't have. But it's still nice to think he actually failed with at least one invention.

THE POLLOCK TWINS

The idea of reincarnation has been around for most of human history and remains a tenet of several major world religions. But could two girls be reincarnated in the same family with just a year between them?

Hexham, England, May 1957. Eleven-year-old Joanna Pollock and her sister, six-year-old Jacqueline, were on their way to church with their friend Anthony when they were hit by a car. The girls were killed instantly, and Anthony died on his way to the hospital.

It was later revealed that the driver was a local woman who deliberately killed the girls after her own kids had been taken away from her. She had previously spent time in psychiatric care after attempting to take her own life.

The Pollock girls' parents, Florence and John, ran a milk delivery business and already had four sons when the two daughters arrived. They were devout Catholics and the deaths naturally devastated them. John thought that God may have been punishing him because, as a child, he had been fascinated by reincarnation, which had led him to question his faith.

The family moved 30 miles away and soon after, Florence fell pregnant again. John's childhood feelings were rekindled and he came to believe that Florence would have twins, despite the midwife finding only one heartbeat and neither family having any history of twins being born.

More than that, he believed they would be the reincarnation of his two beautiful daughters.

Florence was shocked and even spoke about divorcing him. But she was even more shocked when she gave birth – to two beautiful girls.

Could it be John was right? First of all, one twin, Gillian, had the same birthmark as Joanna. The other, Jennifer, had a birthmark on her forehead where Jacqueline had a scar. Gillian walked with splayed feet, the same as Joanna, while Jennifer walked the same way as Jacqueline.

They also seemed to instantly recognize "their own" toys. And when the family decided to return to Hexham, the girls were familiar with places they had never been before and neighbours they had never met.

For the Catholic Pollocks this was a huge test of their faith and their marriage, especially as John was convinced and Florence was not. But Florence herself was shaken when she walked in on the twins playing a game.

Jennifer was lying on the floor, her head cradled in Gillian's lap. Gillian said to her, "The blood's coming out of your eyes. That's where the car hit you." In fact, both girls were terrified of cars, once grabbing each other and yelling "The car is coming to get us!" when one drove quickly past. They could also barely be convinced to walk along the pavement, particularly the way to church where Joanna and Jacqueline had been hit.

On another occasion, Gillian pointed to Jennifer's birthmark on her forehead and told her, "That is the mark Jacqueline got when she fell on a bucket" – exactly what had happened.

As the girls grew older, past the ages of their dead siblings, the strange coincidences seemed to stop. Some people have speculated that, even if their parents never spoke about the dead girls around the twins – as they claimed – they may have sent out enough unconscious signals for the girls to pick up on.

But it's worth remembering some of the greatest thinkers in history have believed in reincarnation, from Plato to Mahatma Gandhi. Some of the world's great religions agree. Could it be that the Pollock girls are living proof?

THE VOYNICH MANUSCRIPT

It is 240 pages long and beautifully illustrated. It has been carbon dated to the early fifteenth century. It's written from left to right. And the pictures in it are recognizable – people, plants, astrological figures. It was purchased in 1912 by the rare bookdealer Wilfrid Voynich and now resides at Yale University. And no one has a clue what it says.

The Voynich Manuscript has baffled scholars and codebreakers since Voynich purchased it from the Society of Jesus in the Vatican, which was trying to raise money by selling off bits of its library. Investigations have traced its movements around Europe, sometimes disappearing for many years then returning somewhere else.

What is so baffling is that it is written in code – at least it seems to be code – and that no one, not even the people who solved the Enigma Code, not even supercomputers calculating millions of algorithms a second, can make head nor tail of it.

If it's not a code, then what? Shorthand has been suggested. Or could it be an example of steganography, as first mentioned by the occultist Johannes Trithemius back in 1499, where a grille is put over a manuscript and only the letters in the holes are relevant. But the irregular nature of the writing makes it unlikely.

A natural lost language? Remarkably computers have found it shares most characteristics of a natural language, and that it is "mostly compatible with natural languages and incompatible with random texts". Which makes a hoax unlikely.

Whatever it is, the Voynich Manuscript continues to baffle and excite all who try and unlock its secrets.

"IT'S NOT AN AIRCRAFT"

It was at 7.06 p.m. when air traffic control in Melbourne, Australia, got the call. A young amateur pilot was on a flight towards King Island in the Bass Strait, between the mainland and Tasmania, and he informed them that he was being accompanied by an aircraft about 1,000 miles above him.

Air traffic control informed the pilot that there were no known flights in that area and at that altitude. The pilot, Frederick Valentich, told them he could definitely see one, and that it seemed to be illuminated by four lights underneath, as though its landing lights were on. Air traffic control repeated, "No known aircraft in the vicinity."

Valentich's voice became increasingly panicked. "It's approaching right now from due east towards me... It seems to me that he's playing some sort of game. He's flying over me two, three times at speeds I could not identify."

Air traffic control asked Valentich if he was able to describe the aircraft. He replied, "As it's flying past, it's a long shape... Cannot identify more than... It's before me right now, Melbourne."

According to Valentich it then started to orbit him, displaying a green light and then vanishing and reappearing. He asked air traffic control if it could be a military aircraft. They asked him again if the aircraft kept coming and going.

There was a pause and Frederick Valentich said, "It's not an aircraft." It was the last air traffic control heard from him.

What had Valentich seen up there? And what had it done to him? Ufologists were quick to identify that what happened to Valentich, while unique, was not without factors in common with many reports of encounters with extra-terrestrials. In particular the green light, which a number of individuals who claim to have come into contact with unidentified flying objects had also mentioned. The way that he described the aircraft hovering was also consistent with other encounters.

Others noted that during World War Two there was a spate of aircraft disappearances in an area very near to where Valentich had been – in fact, some people referred to it as the Bass Strait Triangle. And just six years before Valentich's disappearance another light aircraft had gone missing – without sending any distress signals.

After Valentich disappeared, a huge search operation was launched, covering over 1,000 miles, but nothing was found.

But the following morning the strangest thing happened. A farmer in nearby Cape Otway, on the edge of Valentich's flight path, observed an object hovering above his property. It was 22 yards across and, according to the farmer, had a small plane attached to its side, leaking oil.

The farmer was so baffled by what he saw that he took a screwdriver and etched the aircraft's tail number into one of his tractors so he wouldn't forget it. The object sped away.

The number was the same as Valentich's Cessna.

BABA VANGA

There have been many famous psychics, clairvoyants and fortune-tellers, from the Scottish medium Daniel Dunglas Home in the nineteenth century, who could supposedly levitate and speak with the dead, to the "Sleeping Prophet" Edgar Cayce in the early twentieth century, who could go into a trance and communicate with the spirit world, to Uri Geller in our own time, who allegedly could do anything from bending spoons to influencing the results of football matches through telekinesis. Each of them was a showman, combining their purported supernatural skills with providing entertainment.

But perhaps the most formidable psychic in recent times was Baba Vanga, a small, semi-literate Bulgarian woman.

Born premature in 1911, she was not named until it was certain she would survive. An intelligent girl, she started experimenting with herbs when young and might have lived a quiet life like her family and friends, if not for an amazing incident which happened when she was 14.

A tornado hit her town and swept young Vanga up and dropped her in the middle of a field. Her eyes were covered in dust and she could not open them because of the pain. She had lost her sight – but she had gained what psychics call "second sight".

In a school for the blind she learned Braille in Serbian, but she had to return home on the death of her stepmother and didn't finish her education. She gained a reputation for soothsaying. People would ask her whether any missing relatives were alive or dead. So accurate were her predictions that even Tsar of Bulgaria, Boris III paid a visit.

As Baba Vanga's profile grew she began making predictions not just about the people who came to see her. Over the years she would come to predict the break-up of the Soviet Union, the September 11 attacks ("The American brethren will fall after being attacked by the steel birds... innocent blood will be gushing"), even the exact date of Stalin's death. She also purportedly predicted Princess Diana's passing and the appalling Chernobyl disaster.

The General Secretary of the Soviet Union Leonid Brezhnev paid her a visit – hopefully she was too tactful to mention there would only be three more leaders after him!

So popular was Baba Vanga – who some people now called the Nostradamus of the Balkans – that the Bulgarian government took her under its wing and gave her a secretary to write down her predictions. These included that the 44th president of the United States would be an African-American, and that the 45th would have a "messianic personality" which would "bring the country down". She had already been dead for 12 years when Barack Obama was elected. And we all know who came next.

She had even predicted when her death would be, and so felt no fear as it approached. Just as she reported to her followers many years earlier, she died on 11 August 1996 and was buried two days later. Before she died she told her followers that her gift would be passed on to a ten-year-old French girl, who would become known to everyone in due course.

Recent studies have estimated that over 80 per cent of her predictions have come true, and who knows, some others may still prove that she knew more than any of the rest of us. For instance, one of her final predictions baffled her secretary Neshka Robeva at the time and continued to for many years. Speaking in 2021, Ms Robeva revealed what Baba Vanga had said to her in 1996.

"Neshka, the Corona will be all over us."

FINAL WORD

Can there ever be a final word when it comes to the occult, the supernatural, the paranormal? Throughout human history there have been those who delved into mystery and reported on its wonders. Others have tried to convince us that nothing is "out there", but every answer seems to lead to a million more questions, even more puzzling than the first answer.

After thousands of years there are still reports of extra-terrestrial visits, peculiar deaths, men and women bending time and space to their will. Some can seemingly look far into the future, some deep into the past, others can see both at the same time, read the runes and be initiated into the secret knowledge once only accessible to the gods.

Perhaps you have that power too, perhaps you have already used it. From putting out streetlights to embracing the strange effects of your own Etiäinen walking just a little bit ahead of you, you too may have the power to embrace the occult and make it your own.

Maybe one of these stories has chimed with you, and behind the horror you can recognize yourself, your friends or loved ones, or the things that have happened to you. Perhaps after reading this book, you'll start to notice them more.

FINAL WORD

Because arguably there is no "paranormal world". There is just our world, and it may just all be paranormal to those of us with eyes to see.

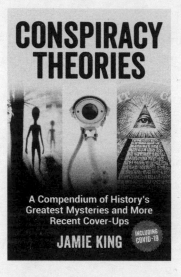

CONSPIRACY THEORIES

A Compendium of History's Greatest Mysteries and More Recent Cover-Ups

Jamie King

ISBN: 978-1-78783-565-8

Where did the Coronavirus outbreak originate and was the pandemic predicted? Did aliens help to build the Sphinx and the Great Pyramid of Giza, and what were they trying to tell us? Is the food industry colluding to make us addicted to sugar? Prepare yourself for some startling revelations on these topics and many more in this updated and expanded compendium of the world's scariest and strangest conspiracy theories.

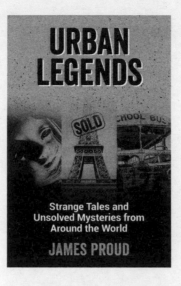

URBAN LEGENDS
Strange Tales and Unsolved Mysteries Around the World

James Proud

ISBN: 978-1-80007-106-3

Strange happenings, unsolved mysteries and seemingly supernatural events have gripped and shocked us for centuries, passed from person to person in whispers in classrooms, tales around the campfire and idle gossip among friends. Whether they're based on a grain of truth or a complete flight of fancy, the myths, legends and weird tales contained within this book will take you on a fascinating journey to the outer limits of plausibility, and dare you to believe the unbelievable.

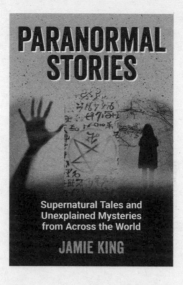

PARANORMAL STORIES

Supernatural Tales and Unexplained Mysteries from Across the World

Jamie King

ISBN: 978-1-80007-189-6

Tales of the paranormal have seduced us and spooked us for centuries, passed around from person to person and frequently retold and reimagined in books, films and TV. Whether they're based on real events or they're simply urban legends which have taken on a life of their own, the strange happenings, unexplained events and unsolved mysteries in this book will take you on a frightening journey to the outer limits of plausibility, and dare you to believe the unbelievable.

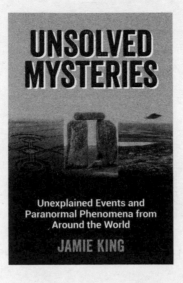

UNSOLVED MYSTERIES
Unexplained Events and Paranormal Phenomena from Around the World

Jamie King

ISBN: 978-1-80007-990-8

Intriguing, captivating and downright bizarre, this heart-pounding collection of unexplained events is guaranteed to keep you up at night. Throughout history, unsolved mysteries have left us searching for answers.

Baffling stories of strange happenings and seemingly supernatural events mean we are terrified of what we can't understand. Theories and folklore surround these events, but as we look for a rational explanation, perhaps the truth might be even more sinister.

Have you enjoyed this book?

If so, find us on Facebook at **Summersdale Publishers**,
on Twitter at **@Summersdale** and on
Instagram and TikTok at **@summersdalebooks**
and get in touch. We'd love to hear from you!

www.summersdale.com